Teacher Well-being

All teachers experience negative stress in the workplace, whether it is due to pressures of the job whilst at school or to the perpetual need to take work home. In this informative book, Elizabeth Holmes provides practical advice and solutions to enable teachers to experience less negative stress in their life and to understand the links between the way they function in the classroom and their personal well-being.

Providing strategies for teachers wanting to be proactive in dealing with their well-being, stress and career, and drawing on real-life case-studies, this book outlines all the different components that contribute to physical, emotional, spiritual and mental well-being. This includes:

- Good stress and bad stress
- Communication
- Enhancing personal well-being at school
- Well-being and career development

Written in a clear and accessible style with plenty of practical examples and advice, *Teacher Well-being* is essential reading for all teachers, headteachers and school managers, whether just entering the profession or experienced practitioners.

Elizabeth Holmes is a freelance writer and researcher. She is the author of *The Newly Qualified Teacher's Handbook*, also published by RoutledgeFalmer. **Elizabeth Holmes** is also the on-line agony aunt for the teacher recruitment website Eteach.com.

Teacher Well-being

Looking after yourself and your career in the classroom

Elizabeth Holmes

 RoutledgeFalmer
Taylor & Francis Group

LONDON AND NEW YORK

For Maisie Elizabeth Browne

First published 2005 by RoutledgeFalmer
2 Park Square, Milton Park, Abingdon, Oxon OX14 4RN

Simultaneouly published in the USA and Canada
by RoutledgeFalmer
270 Madison Ave, New York, NY 10016

RoutledgeFalmer is an imprint of the Taylor & Francis Group

© 2005 Elizabeth Holmes

The right of Elizabeth Holmes to be identified as the Author of
this Work has been asserted by her in accordance with the Copyright,
Designs and Patents Act 1988

Typeset in Garamond and Gill by BC Typesetting Ltd, Bristol
Printed and bound in Great Britain by
MPG Books Ltd., Bodmin, Cornwall

British Library Cataloguing in Publication Data
A catalogue record for this book is available from the British Library

Library of Congress Cataloging in Publication Data
Holmes, Elizabeth Anne, 1969–
     Teacher well-being: looking after yourself and your career in the
     classroom/Elizabeth Holmes. – 1st ed.
          p.   cm.
     Includes bibliographical references and index.
     ISBN 0–415–33498–5 (pbk.: alk. paper) 1. Teachers – Job Stress.
     2. Teachers – Mental Health. 3. Teaching – Psychological aspects.
     4. Stress Management. I. Title.
     LB2840.2.H65 2004
     371.1′001′9–dc22

                                                          2004004778

ISBN 0–415–33498–5

Contents

Acknowledgements

This book, from conception to delivery, was several years in the making. During that time I was fortunate to meet and speak to many teachers and school leaders about their experiences of negative stress and their pursuit of well-being. I am extremely grateful for the time, insights, thoughts and inspirations that were so freely given. Thanks must also go to Kevin McCarthy of Re:membering Education and numerous health practitioners of various kinds, including those at the Institute for Optimum Nutrition, for invaluable input as I attempted to tame unruly thoughts about what well-being can actually encompass.

Several editors worked with me on the plans for this book before the first word had been typed. Emma Martin, Jonathan Simpson and Steve Jones all had a positive influence on its development in those early stages, and I'm also particularly grateful to Philip Mudd of RoutledgeFalmer and Charlotte Howard of Fox and Howard Literary Agency, whose enthusiastic encouragement provided the impetus to get this book written and out there! In addition I'm grateful to Kelly Hallett and the rest of the RoutledgeFalmer team who contributed to its publication.

I would also like to thank Patrick Nash, Corrina Cordon and the team at the Teacher Support Network, and Hetty Meyric-Hughes at www. teachernet.gov.uk, who gave such positive feedback prior to publication.

Finally, my thanks go to my family and friends, whose unfailing support contributes immeasurably to my own well-being.

Foreword

Teacher stress is a major problem. It damages lives, ends careers and affects teaching standards.

Numerous studies since the 1980's have demonstrated what, to many parents and to almost all teachers, is a self-evident problem. And yet, it was not until the late 1990's that employers, government and policy makers began to acknowledge it.

The Teacher Support Network established Teacher Support Line (formerly Teacherline) in 1999 in response to this. Since then, we have received tens of thousands of calls from teachers – helping them to solve their problems before they get out of hand. Year on year, the number of teachers contacting us increases and we are making an impact where it matters – helping teachers to feel supported, confident, listened to and valued, so that they can enjoy and do well at their jobs. Confidential counselling is allowing teachers to address and resolve issues such as anxiety and depression, conflict, workload, pupil behaviour and job dissatisfaction. And our experience shows that teachers want to resolve these problems that create stress and are very open to finding their own solutions.

But the health and well-being of the teachers in our schools isn't just the responsibility of the individual concerned. There is much that schools, heads, LEAs and Government could and should be doing. A good example of another positive step being taken is the Well-Being Programme. Run by Worklife Support (a social enterprise originally established by the Teacher Support Network), the Well-Being Programme is a nationwide initiative that encourages schools to become healthy and well-functioning working and learning environments. It is already having a significant impact in dozens of LEAs across the country.

It is encouraging to see that this book raises awareness of the health and well-being issues that teachers encounter – and gives practical advice as to how these issues can be addressed. We are delighted that Elizabeth Holmes has written it and are sure it will provide readers with inspiration and guidance.

Patrick Nash
Chief Executive, Teacher Support Network

Introduction

There can be few teachers who do not have a solid understanding of what negative stress means, born of genuine felt experience. If it is not the pressures of the job whilst at school, it is the perpetual need to take work home that eats into our sense of control and overall job satisfaction. Clearly, there is a delicate balance to be found between the buzz of the opportunities that the teaching profession can offer, through new initiatives and ideas such as teacher creativity and citizenship, and negative stress and burnout.

Alarming levels of stress as well as of depression among teachers have been reported in recent years, in particular by Teacher Support Line, the counselling, support and advice service set up in England and Wales to help teachers who are struggling through the impact of negative stress. It is because of this that attention within the profession is increasingly turning to the notion of supporting teachers before stress takes hold, rather than waiting until the need for active stress management is so great as to necessitate immediate action.

Leading on from this tendency towards proaction come the ideas behind teachers' well-being. If we can divide the concept of well-being into the different 'wells' of physical, spiritual, emotional and intellectual/mental health, it is possible to hold negative stress responsible for 'dis-ease' in just about every dimension of our lives.

That there should be increasing awareness of teachers' stress and well-being can only be a good thing. There are obvious links between a teaching force that is in balance, working within healthy parameters of pressure, and the success and achievements of the pupils they teach. Yet we should guard against making too much of these connections. Looking after teachers' well-being should be honourable enough as a goal without needing to use improvements in pupil performance as an excuse for its priority.

In recent years there have been some high-profile court cases relating to teacher stress. Record damages have been awarded to teachers who buckled under the pressures imposed on them. In each of these cases, a persistent lack of practical support from those who should have been monitoring the experiences of the teachers greatly contributed to the severity of the suffering experienced.

This is perhaps one of the most intriguing aspects of the teaching profession. We can be devoted, sometimes beyond the call of duty, to the well-being of our pupils, but when it comes to nurturing each other the picture is not always so positive. Yet we should not dwell for too long on the shortfalls of the systems currently in place to prevent teacher burnout, lest we never break free from reacting to the events we face in our working lives. Rather, we should be embracing the responsibility that each of us has for our own well-being. If this is to be achieved, many in the profession will have to undertake profound changes to their practice, preferably removing any element of self-sacrifice and over-conscientiousness from their daily work.

The inherent tension between the individual and institutional approaches to teacher well-being is ever present in the profession. Who should accept full responsibility? *Teacher Well-being* does not seek to provide an answer to this question; nor does it lay out a stress management policy that can slot on to the shelf among other school policies. Neither does it present a specific and limited goal for you to pursue. It does, however, seek to engage the reader in committing to an investment in what could ultimately ease any negative stress and promote a sustainable sense of well-being. This is surely an investment paying the highest dividends.

Perhaps now is a good time to mention self-help books. Love them or hate them, they have become in recent years a powerful genre in the world of publishing. If you are at all irritated by their style and content, this book seeks to differ in at least one important respect: that of application. As the book is specific to the teaching profession, it is hoped that the ideas can be applied (or modified to apply) to the situations you might find yourself facing at work. It is also my hope that we might appreciate the extent to which stress aids our survival through the energy, arousal and drive it gives us to adapt to external stimuli. But it should be noted that all the hints, tips and ideas are just that. They are not a prescription for a stress-free life. If something sits well with you, try it. If it doesn't, leave it for a while and perhaps revisit another time. Not everything can work for everyone, but if you would like to contribute your thoughts on teachers' stress and well-being you can e-mail me at: eh@elizabethholmes.co.uk. The first edition of any book is a starting-point from which it can grow and develop. Feedback from those who read and use this book can help this process immeasurably.

As I visit schools and talk to teachers and headteachers across the country, it is clear that perceptions of negative stress in the profession vary tremendously. Some seem complacent about the inroads they are making in tackling this dis-ease, while others seem unnecessarily self-critical. Some scoff at stress-busting ideas, while colleagues in neighbouring schools think nothing of embracing fully the range of treatments and techniques that currently exist. There will naturally be an element of trial and error involved when building up a personal store of stress-busting tools; what might work at any one time must *feel* right for the moment. But what should always be remembered is that *something* will work for you. It may take a while to understand your reactions and responses to events and pressures, but there is the potential for all stress-related problems to have solutions.

I view negative stress in life and in work as being one of the biggest threats to the development of human potential and the release of creativity. It is this release that can promote true improvements in the quality of life that we experience; and, as concepts, well-being and quality of life cannot be separated. For this reason, stress in the teaching profession is one of life's ironies; perhaps greater than we have ever appreciated.

I wish you well in your quest for work–life equilibrium. While I would hope that this book might assist you in the short-term management of any negative stress you might be experiencing, my greater desire is that this coping might be just the first step in your journey towards a holistic and long-term relationship with life-enriching balance in your work.

- *Checklists.* For ease of information retrieval, many ideas have been organised into lists. They have been written to help inspire your own solutions to stress-related issues, and should not be regarded as exhaustive. They are a time-saving device to dip into, select the information you need, and go.
- *'Action' features.* These features seek to offer the opportunity to draw from your wealth of resources for problem-solving. They have also been written to enable you to experience stress-busting techniques, and to work through where stress may be centred in your life. Work

through them when it seems appropriate, but there will be no need to complete them all.

- *'Example' features*. All of the examples are real experiences, although names have been excluded. They are there to illustrate points in the text, and some deal with relatively unusual situations.
- *'About' boxes*. These boxes contain succinct information covering many issues connected to negative stress and teacher well-being.

Read this book slowly and carefully, or 'flick and dip'. The choice is yours!

Author's note

Any advice given in this book concerning the health of a reader is for information and guidance only, and is not intended to replace the advice of a qualified healthcare practitioner. Symptoms of stress, in particular, require extremely careful management, and while self-treatment can help tremendously it is always wise to have such symptoms registered with your chosen healthcare provider. Neither the author nor the publisher can be held responsible for any consequences that occur as a result of following the guidance contained herein.

Whatever path of action you find that brings good and happiness to all, follow this way like the moon in the path of the stars.

(*The Dharma School, Brighton*)

CHAPTER I

All about well-being

Well-being: the state of being comfortable, healthy or happy
(The New Oxford Dictionary of English)

As a teacher, you are expending your energy educating, dealing with, caring for, nurturing and encouraging young people. At some level at least, you know that this is worthwhile even when the job feels overwhelming and the balance of your life needs attention. In fact, this knowledge probably has a good deal to do with why you went into the profession in the first place. Teachers often feel – know – that investing this energy, time and attention in pupils will bring them closer to achieving their potential. But the bottom line is that the job, and all it entails, can both sustain you and exhaust you.

If the job does exhaust you, is that just too bad? If you can't stand the pace of classroom life, should you simply leave? Is that it? Not quite! We don't live in a barbarian society where a 'survival of the fittest' mentality prevails. We know that 'results', and all the connotations a word like that carries in our world, are dependent on a wide variety of factors, and that those who do not have a sense of well-being in their life are less able to contribute to their full potential. To ignore this is to risk immense loss. Loss to ourselves, to those we teach, to our communities and, ultimately, to the world.

Bringing this right down to its most basic level, it would not be outrageous to recognise that the well-being of the teachers in our schools is intimately connected to pupil performance. Even if we only partially believe this to be true, healthy practices which foster well-being need to be embedded deep within the culture of a school.

But what exactly is this supposed key to success?

The following is intended to serve as a brief introduction to the notion of well-being and its various components. Focus, both implicit and explicit, will be given to each element as appropriate throughout the book.

Well-being defined

> Remembering ourselves and our power can lead to revolution, but it requires more than recalling a few facts. *Re-membering* involves putting ourselves back together, recovering identity and integrity, reclaiming the wholeness of our lives.
>
> (Parker J Palmer, *The Courage to Teach*, p. 20)

Well-being is a vague expression, bordering on the indefinable, yet claiming an increasingly dominant place in our psyche. We may not fully grasp all that it entails, but we know we want to make sure we get our fair share; it sounds that good. There's even a 'well-being' aisle in most supermarkets now, and a well-known florist is selling a 'well-being bouquet', so if commerce is jumping on the bandwagon it must be seeping into the public consciousness!

Well-being requires harmony between mind and body. It implies a sense of balance and ease with the myriad dimensions of life. When we feel a sense of well-being, we are not under-stimulated and bored, nor are we suffering under the burden of excessive stress and pressure. We have a sense of control over our work and even over our destiny in life.

Historically, the mind-and-body connection has been rejected by some aspects of modern medicine. Yet, increasingly, studies are showing the extent of the influence that the mind can have over physical and emotional dis-ease. If we want to consider our personal well-being, we have to recognise that it is not simply the opposite of stress, just as health is not the opposite of sickness. There is far more to the concept than that.

ACTION What's your immediate reaction to what you have read so far about the notion of well-being?

Do you have any instinctive feelings about the degree of well-being that you are currently experiencing in your life?

EXAMPLE BREAKING DOWN

For many years I have worked under the illusion that because I was healthy, needed very few days of sick leave and could always be relied on to cover other people's classes I was somehow stronger than my colleagues. I couldn't understand why so many of them seemed to limp through each term. But, then, I led a relatively uncomplicated life. It was only when my mother died that the veneer of 'coping' that I had perfected over the years started to crumble and I saw overwhelming problems in just about every aspect of life. I should have paced myself differently throughout my career. I should have looked not just at me the super-efficient teacher, but at me the whole person. Yes, I'm still a teacher, despite what can only be described as a breakdown; but, if you were to ask me what well-being is, I could answer with real knowledge and experience of what it feels like to be so dangerously out of kilter. It's not necessarily the strongest physically and emotionally that never need time off. It's not necessarily these people who are experiencing well-being.

(Secondary teacher with twenty years' experience)

Defining the scope of well-being

The scope of well-being is wide and deep, and may well vary depending on the perspective from which you are exploring the issue. For the purposes of defining the scope of well-being both in the classroom and in the wider context of life, we can divide it into the following sub-categories:

- physical well-being
- emotional well-being
- mental and intellectual well-being
- spiritual well-being

The needs of each sub-category are explored implicitly throughout the book, and advice on promoting each one within the context of school life is given. However, while the intrinsic elements of well-being can be extracted from the concept, it's important to take a holistic approach to it, which is why there are no systematic prescriptions to be found here!

Physical well-being

Physical well-being encompasses all aspects of our physical being. The shape we're in, our ability to resist disease, the exercise we get, the food we eat, and so on, all contribute to our physical well-being. It is far more than simply the absence of sickness or disease.

In many ways, physical well-being is our ultimate challenge. Not only is modern life so hectic that time can rarely be found truly to focus on our physical bodies and the needs we may have, but we are also under attack from toxins and pollutants in our food and water and in the air we breathe.

Yet it is important not to feel that we are powerless in determining our physical well-being. One of the most significant factors in our physical health is the finely balanced relationship between mind and body. We can categorise different aspects of well-being, but we cannot lose sight of the deep interrelationships between them.

EXAMPLE A NEED FOR EXERCISE

At a recent doctor's appointment I was asked how much exercise I got. I burst out laughing. I'm a reception teacher, so it's hardly as if I do a sedentary job! But the fact is I've put on weight since I've been doing this job and I was sitting in front of my GP who I knew was about to tell me to join a gym or start jogging in my rare spare moments. He actually used the words 'physical well-being' and told me I'd be able to cope with my work more effectively if my general levels of fitness were improved. I had to swallow my pride and take it, but it's very tough to hear. I feel self-indulgent even thinking about it, but the stark reality is that, if I don't keep an eye on my physical well-being, it doesn't matter how great I am with the kids, I simply won't be around to do my job.

(Primary teacher with ten years' experience)

ACTION When you consider the term 'physical well-being' what's your reaction?

Do you consider it has to take a priority in your life?

Are you able to see that it's possible to view your physical being as separate in some way from other dimensions of your being?

Should your physical well-being receive targeted treatment?

How would you define your overall attitude to your physical well-being?

Emotional well-being

We all experience an emotional life. In fact, the way in which we interact in the world is, to a great extent, dependent upon our emotional response to the events we face from day to day.

Adults are mostly aware of their emotions but may not always be fully in control of them. They are central to the decisions we make and the way that we respond to the world. We even find ourselves dealing with the fallout from others' emotional responses day in, day out, especially where pupils are concerned.

While sound relationships will help to contribute greatly to the emotional well-being of all members of a school's community, there must also be an appreciation of the power that emotions have in directing an individual's life. The ability to recognise, understand and appropriately express emotions is a valuable key to emotional well-being.

Emotional intelligence (sometimes referred to as emotional literacy)

It would be impossible now to mention a term such as 'emotional well-being' without at least tentatively exploring the work of key thinkers in the realm of emotional intelligence.

The term 'emotional intelligence' was first coined by Daniel Goleman in 1995 in his book *Emotional Intelligence*. Charting the work of the psychologist Peter Salovey, Goleman identifies skills such as recognising and handling one's own emotions, being motivated, productive and efficient, having the ability to recognise others' emotions empathetically, and being capable of sustaining relationships as some of the essential components of emotional intelligence. Going back a decade earlier, it's possible to see how these capacities are reflected in the work of another seminal writer in this field, the psychologist Howard Gardner, who tentatively identified seven intelligences:

- linguistic
- logical-mathematical
- spatial
- musical
- bodily-kinaesthetic
- interpersonal
- intrapersonal

Few teachers have received any formal training in these areas, yet some manage them very well for much of the time, whether through formal education or out of a natural affinity with the concepts involved. There is little doubt, however, that when we take this kind of development seriously there are untold benefits to be had personally as well as for our pupils in the classroom.

The team of researchers who wrote *Learning by Heart: the role of emotional learning in raising school achievement* concluded that:

- understanding emotions is directly connected with motivation and with cognitive achievement
- dealing with emotions helps to develop better relationships and a sense of psychological and mental well-being
- emotionally developed people are better equipped to live with difference
- educating the emotions leads to a more effective workforce
- our moral outlook and value systems are deeply shaped by our attitudes and feelings
- our sense of meaning and purpose is derived as much from feeling as from understanding

Those with physical challenges can still tutor others on how to perfect their skills as an athlete or a dancer. They don't have to be able to perform the moves themselves to know how someone else should in order to improve their expertise. Someone with weight to lose can teach another about the basic fundamentals of a healthy diet. The same does not apply to emotional realms. Those who are not on top of who they are emotionally, what affects their emotional well-being and how to move themselves towards rebalancing their emotional life are clearly not equipped to help others to do the same. There is a distinct difference between the two.

EXAMPLE EMOTIONALLY SHY

Oh God, how I groan whenever I hear the terms 'emotion', 'emotional', 'emotional literacy' or whatever else it's embroiled in! I cringe when I'm asked stuff like that. I'm a man! I'm not supposed to be comfortable using language like that! I know it's a cliché and there are loads of men out there far more comfortable with it all than I am, but, really, can we just leave it? I'm a teacher, not a psychologist. Have I just let the side down?

(Secondary teacher with five years' experience)

ACTION Picture the scene. It's a wild and windy afternoon, the last of the week, and you're covering a colleague's class at short notice with no resources and no lesson plan. They're not exactly brimming with enthusiasm about the fact that you're with them, and you're having to exert control and discipline far more than you're comfortable with.

Having finally settled them, with equipment loaned and borrowed, seating 'negotiated' and a modicum of quiet in the room, you're able to introduce the lesson and set out what needs to be done. Not five minutes into this period of relative calm, you and the class are aware of shouting in the corridor. An altercation between a teacher and a pupil by the sound of it. A minute or so later the door bursts open, flies back on its hinges, and in tumbles Jo(e) who scowls to his/her place, slams a more or less empty bag on the desk and sprawls with deliberate provocation on a chair.

What happens next?

Do you visualise a best or a worst scenario?

What would the best and worst scenarios be?

What state do you imagine your emotional well-being would be in?

The way in which the following minutes pan out is largely dependent upon what has become known as the emotional intelligence of the teacher, the student and, to some extent, the school.

Mental and intellectual well-being

Mental and intellectual well-being is perhaps even harder to define than emotional well-being, but for the purposes of this book it should be taken to refer to the mindset that encourages continuing professional and personal development. It does not refer to the traditional definitions of mental health but, rather, relates to those factors which must be present if you are to feel a sense of intellectual well-being throughout the course of your work.

The mental and intellectual well-being of teachers is closely linked to emotional well-being. There may well be emotional factors which block your attitude towards the stimulation you receive at work, and the professional learning that you may or may not have the opportunity to complete. If your school is not particularly effective at actively promoting the mental and intellectual well-being of its staff members, either implicitly, through the way in which it functions as an institution, or explicitly, through the interest that is taken in your professional learning, mental and intellectual well-being can suffer.

EXAMPLE DEVELOPING PROFESSIONALLY

Looking back, I can see that I had virtually ground to a halt. My lessons were dull, I'd be the first to admit that, and I had no interest in revamping them so that they better suited the kids I was teaching. But in my defence I'd had no opportunities to learn from other teachers, to observe others at work, to go on courses (there was never any money for that) or just to talk to someone about how I was functioning at work. It was like being in a lonely void, and I'll always be grateful for my current headteacher who took me on when I know I wasn't exactly in my most dynamic phase! I've now been on courses, I've observed others, I regularly check in on the virtual Staffroom on www.eteach.com and I feel totally re-inspired in my work. If I had forgotten what I was doing in the profession, I've certainly remembered now. I'm not sure I could define for you exactly what I understand by mental and intellectual well-being, but I know for certain what it feels like without it. Those feelings of despondency creep up on you, and you have to do something to snap out of it. Incredibly hard to do, but essential if you want to cling to your sanity at work!

(Secondary teacher with fifteen years' experience)

ACTION As you read through this chapter, are you able to start to identify with the breakdown of various elements of 'well-being' as a notion?

Have you ever thought about your mental and intellectual well-being as a distinct element of your overall well-being?

What care do you take at the moment to ensure that your mental and intellectual well-being is supported?

Spiritual well-being

Embedded deep within the English National Curriculum is the aim that schools should promote pupils' spiritual, moral, social and cultural development. Pupils' spiritual well-being is a priority, and teachers are charged with seeing to it that pupils are adequately prepared for life as far as their spiritual well-being is concerned – but what on earth is it?

The most significant thing to remember when considering the notion of spiritual well-being is that that term 'spirit' need not be connected with religion or even with some realm above and beyond the here and now. There are no prerequisites to spiritual well-being, no need to belong to a specific tradition and no pretence to enlightenment. Of course, it is usually central to the world's main religions, but not 'belonging' does not preclude you from developing a sense of nurturing and sustaining spiritual well-being. The point has been made before, but is worth reiterating here, that spiritual well-being is not dependent upon religious belief.

You will almost certainly have your own understanding of what spiritual well-being means for you, and this is far more important, and will serve you far better, than any ideas put forward here. If, however, you don't have a definition that works for you, these ideas may help.

Writers in the past have described spiritual well-being and the human desire to pursue it as evidence of our need to experience that which extends beyond the material world. It has also been linked with the desire to become in some way a fuller, more rounded person, as if an ability to recognise and nurture spiritual well-being will help to engender creative freedom in life and a willingness to go beyond previously imposed boundaries. With spiritual well-being comes the ability to be constructively self-conscious and self-critical when a sense of a greater good is being pursued.

EXAMPLE SPIRITUALLY SHY

I don't go to church. There's nothing in my life that could be termed 'spiritual'. Do you mean New Age stuff? I don't see how it can relate to school. Perhaps, if I was religious, I might. Isn't all that stuff kind of private?

(Primary teacher with five years' experience)

Spirituality has also been described as a thread running through our lives offering purpose and meaning, courage and peace, as if extending beyond the everyday, beyond what we can see and what we can touch. Ultimately, spirituality can serve as an ever-present source of inspiration helping us to live and work with integrity, compassion, connection, enthusiasm, meaning and vision – to name but a few!

EXAMPLE LIFTING SPIRITS

When I get a group of my worst 15-year-olds to grasp a mathematical concept, that gives my spiritual well-being a boost. I get a kick out of it. When they want to know more, despite the challenges that are going on in their lives, I know that there's meaning in what I'm doing. When the guy who's a known non-attender turns up, albeit late and in a foul mood, and actually gets something from the lesson, who leaves the room saying 'That was well cool, sir,' my spirit is lifted. Even if I only get that feeling a few times each term, it's enough to feed on.

(Secondary teacher with ten years' experience)

We either make ourselves miserable, or we make ourselves strong. The amount of work is the same.

(Carlos Casteneda)

Whether you realise it or not, there are no boundaries, but until you realise it, you cannot manifest it. The limitations that each one of us has are defined in the ways we use our minds.

(John Daido Loori)

EXAMPLE SPIRITUAL WELL-BEING

I'm not embarrassed to admit that I do feel a spiritual connection to all that I do in school. In fact, it pervades my entire life. I don't think other people know that about me, and this is probably the first time I've actually arranged my thoughts on this into words. I think I view my spiritual well-being as being able to find meaning in what I do. It's nothing outrageously egotistical, but just a knowledge that what I'm doing is part of a larger picture. I think it relates mostly to my sense of purpose and the values I choose to live by. For me, there has to be a connection to my spiritual life. It's how I can make meaning out of what happens to me and gives me a sort of philosophical handle on life. This has been incredibly useful to me in the classroom. I've never doubted that I want to be a teacher, that I am a teacher, but when the going gets tough I know that I tune into the spiritual side of me and draw strength from my beliefs. Put it this way: there are many methods I use to ensure that I don't ever lose sight of my spiritual well-being. If I did, I know I wouldn't be able to do the job. It cannot be a remote concept for me. I need it to be ever-present in my life and to always remember that there are no ordinary moments.

(Primary teacher with three years' experience)

ACTION Does it mean anything to you, or would you prefer to run a mile from the idea of spiritual well-being?

Can you identify in your life where you are inspired by a sense of the spiritual?

Does this inspiration affect you in your work?

Can you think of moments when you have experienced what you might call spiritual well-being even if it's not a term you'd usually use?

Think of phrases such as 'team spirit', 'being spirited', 'feeling in high or low spirits', 'the spirit of adventure', 'spirit of nature', 'the spirit of competition', 'creative spirit' and so on. Have you ever experienced any of these?

Do you have a sense of what increases spiritual well-being for you both at work and at home?

Can you identify what sometimes threatens your spiritual well-being – again, both at work and at home?

ABOUT WELL-BEING AND ITS RELATIONSHIP TO SCHOOLS

A recent conference organised by the Teacher Support Network in England explored the concept of teacher well-being and staff retention in schools. Some facts to emerge at the conference were:

- Out of every 100 teachers enrolled into teacher education institutes, 40 drop out of their course, 15 move into another branch of education and 10 leave after just three years of teaching. Hence, on average, only about a third remain in teaching as a full-time career.
- According to recent UK government figures, a teacher taking sick leave was absent for ten days during the year on average.
- Staff turnover can cost schools in the UK £40,000 a year.
- 49 per cent of applications for ill-health retirement from education cite psychiatric reasons.

Interestingly, what also emerged at the conference is the fact that there is no single overall answer to the current state of staff retention and teacher well-being. Rather, there ideally needs to be both individual and organisational responses to the issue as pursuing just one route or the other will not improve teacher well-being effectively enough.

Individual counselling has played an important role in keeping teachers in the profession. The Teacher Support Network has assessed feedback from 70,000 people who have used the Teacher Support Line in the UK over the last four years, and this provision of confidential counselling is enabling teachers to handle their jobs better and remain in post.

Organisational approaches to teacher well-being have also been shown to work. From research, we know that teachers remain in their jobs because of the school's management, its ethos and the general morale amongst staff. When teachers are praised, supported and consulted, well-being is higher.

Research from the UK Audit Commission also revealed that it is 'push' not 'pull' factors that trigger teachers to leave their jobs when it comes to teacher well-being. The suggestion has been made that, in order to retain staff, their whole experience of the job must be taken into consideration, hence taking a holistic approach to well-being and all that it might entail.

continued on facing page

Headteachers who are already taking a proactive approach to the well-being of their staff are reporting that it improves health, motivation, recruitment and retention, reduces sick leave and helps to create inclusive communities. This, in turn, has an impact on school culture and effectiveness, staff performance, pupil behaviour, communication and so on.

The Well-Being Programme – Worklife Support from the Teacher Support Network

The Well-Being Programme is a unique programme developed specifically to support schools to enhance the health, well-being and effectiveness of their staff. It gives the whole school team an opportunity to reflect on their school as a workplace, how they organise themselves, how they work together as a team, and the impact this has on everyone who works there.

The programme, which is now effective in almost 1000 schools across 42 Local Education Authorities, helps schools to come together as a team to devise their own unique, practical strategy to create a positive place in which to work. It provides resources and support to unleash the creativity, energy and answers that already lie within their school. That's what makes Well-Being work!

EXAMPLE RETAINING STAFF

The beauty of Well-being (the Well-Being Programme run by Worklife Support from the Teacher Support Network, see above for further details) is that it's all about the staff. If we can't look after the people who look after the children, who's going to look after the children?

I do believe that Well-Being has helped us attract staff and hang on to existing staff. Look at how much it can cost to place an ad. If you can keep the staff you have, it's bound to save money.

I think the programme helps address problems such as burnout. It gives people the confidence to prioritise their workload. If you keep loading people with more work, they end up jaded, tired out. That is put across to their colleagues and the children. They need time to renew and refresh themselves. We are all thoroughly committed to education, to schools and to teaching, but it cannot take over our lives. Yes, people want decent pay, but they also want to work in an environment that looks after them. I've got people out there who are motivated and enthused, and motivating and enthusing, and they love teaching and they want to stay.

(Headteacher taking part in the Well-Being Programme)

ACTION WHAT IS YOUR BLISS?

We all know that there are certain activities, people and places that sustain us, that send us nurturing signals and enhance our sense of overall well-being. But do we always resort to them when our well-being is being rocked? Do we remember them and use them? Not always.

Think of the activities that sustain you, that you know you can rely on to make you feel better. It doesn't matter how simple they are (taking the scenic route home, treating yourself to your favourite chocolate bar, ringing your best friend, going to the gym and so on) as long as you know that they help you to relax and better manage life's challenges.

Write these activities, people and places down. Include details of precisely *how* they restore you and help you to feel great.

In short, what is on your bliss list?

Be sure to look at your bliss list as often as possible. Remind yourself what's on it every day if it helps, and remember that at least one element of your bliss should be a daily priority in your life.

CHAPTER 2

Stress, the good and the bad

Stress: a state of mental or emotional strain or tension resulting from adverse or very demanding circumstances

(The New Oxford Dictionary of English)

It's a phrase we hear all the time, in books, in newspapers, on television; even young children talk in terms of 'being stressed'. Research papers report the damage being done to our 'social environment' by insufficient notice being taken of the stress that employees feel, and the devastating impact this can have on the well-being of individuals is apparently stifling creativity and motivation.

Stress in the workplace is now at record levels, with the number of days lost as a result of work-related stress, anxiety and depression having doubled since 1995. In fact, it is thought to be the primary reason for taking time off work – above, even, common reasons such as backache and colds. Stress also evidently affects our home life, too, with debt and divorce in particular at record levels.

Definitions and perceptions of stress

Perhaps it would be fair to say that stress gets a bad press! But what, exactly, does it mean? Used to describe everything from life-threatening events to situations that merely disrupt our sense of comfort, and a whole array in between, 'stress' has meaning for most, if not all, adults and some children. That said, it's difficult to reach a universally accepted definition. Perhaps it is the fact that we all apply our own meaning to the term that has helped it to become the epidemic of modern life.

Regardless of definitions and perceptions, what is widely accepted is that the states of insufficient stress and excessive stress are both to be avoided if our sense of well-being is to be supported. One useful analogy that is often used compares stress with electricity. A certain amount is needed in order for things to work, but too much and you'll blow them up.

EXAMPLE A PERSONAL VIEW OF STRESS

Stress to me is when I'm scared to write a 'to do' list. It's when my skin breaks out and my hair feels dry. It's invariably when just about everything goes wrong – car, washing machine, you name it! It's when I wake up in the night thinking about lesson plans, marking, meetings, conversations I've had and conversations I should have had. It's feeling distracted when I'm not working and exhausted when I am. That's what stress is to me.

(Primary teacher with five years' experience)

In the 1950s, Dr Hans Seyle distinguished between *eustress* and *distress*. Eustress he described as good, or positive, stress, and distress as bad, or negative, stress. It is impossible to determine exactly where the line between positive and negative stress lies, but self-knowledge can help us to predict it with at least a little certainty.

Positive stress

Positive stress is what motivates us. It's what gives us enough drive, energy and enthusiasm to get a job done, without pushing us into the outer reaches of excessive and damaging stress. When positively stressed, we feel that what we have to do, whether at work or at home, is *achievable*. Not only do we have the ability to be successful, but we also have the means and the time.

Although positive stress still involves demands on our mind and our body, being able to handle these demands, and even to enjoy the challenges they provide, protects us from the ill-effects commonly associated with excessive stress. We feel inspired by the stress facing us and able to respond creatively.

One key point to note is that, while certain events such as bereavement and divorce are clearly going to cause us to experience the negative impact of stress, it is generally our *reaction* to events that determines the extent of the stress felt, rather than the event itself. When there is a balance between what you are expected to do and what you are able to do, your reaction to the demands is more likely to be positive and any stress perceived acts merely as a motivating force.

Your ability to respond to situations so that you are able to remain in the positive stress 'zone' is dependent on a variety of factors. The size of this 'zone' can vary over time, too. Nothing is fixed when it comes to stress!

ABOUT OPTIMUM STRESS

There is such a thing as 'optimum stress'. It occupies the space between the boredom and under-stimulation of too little stress and the excessive burdens of too much stress. Self-knowledge is the only route to consistently interpreting when you are working at optimum stress levels and when you are not.

Negative stress

Negative stress occurs when there is a clear imbalance between what is realistic for you to achieve and what you feel you have to tackle. Stress ceases to be a motivating force in your life, and adverse physical and mental symptoms can arise as a result of the abnormal pressure you perceive.

Feeling negative stress does not necessarily indicate imminent failure. Just because you're up against it does not mean you won't achieve the desired result, but you must be aware of the impact that the negative stress can have on your body and mind. Prolonged negative stress keeps us in a heightened state of 'fight or flight' far longer than we need to be, or than is healthy, so it is essential to take steps to recover from its effects. However we perceive it, the reality is that life is not an on-going emergency.

ACTION What does 'stress' mean to you?

Do you associate it with anxiety, fear, pressure?

What other characteristics does it hold for you? Does it diminish your self-worth? Your self-confidence?

Now take a moment or two to consider what the opposite of 'stress' is for you? What characterises you when you say you do not feel stressed? Is it calm, peace and well-being, or something else?

The stress curve

Figure 2.1 shows the 'stress curve', in other words, what happens to us when we experience too little, the optimum level, and too much stress.

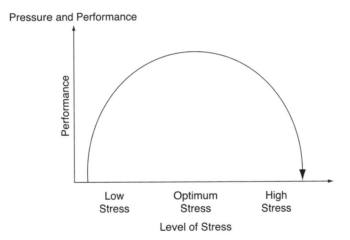

Figure 2.1

Success consists of getting up just one more time than you fall down.
(Oliver Goldsmith)

We all live under the same sky, but we don't all have the same horizon.
(Konrad Adenauer)

ABOUT MEASURING YOUR STRESS

Teacher Support Network runs a fully interactive online multiple-choice assessment of teacher stress. It covers symptoms and signs, work and life events and pressures, and well-being and lifestyle. You can submit your responses online and receive an immediate automatically generated report.

Although this is not intended to provide a comprehensive and systematic personal stress audit, both the process of completing the questionnaire and the report that follows will give you a clear idea of the impact that negative stress is having on your life at the moment.

There is a link to the stress assessment from the homepage of the Teacher Support Network website: www.teachersupport.info

Types of stress

Several thinkers on stress and stress management have categorised the concept of stress, splitting it typically as follows:

- Stress resulting from anticipation: fear of what's to come, worry and anxiety.
- Stress as a response to a current situation: it's happening now, and you have to react.
- Stress from the past: it happened a while ago, but is still large in your mind and seemingly impossible to let go.
- Chronic stress: it's an on-going situation, or reaction to a specific event, the impact of which is lingering.

ACTION Are you able to identify different types of stress in your life?

Which type from the list above would you say you suffer from most?

The physiological stress response

Stress leads to physiological responses in your body. These responses are clear evidence that your body is seeking to maintain homeostasis (or equilibrium), and without them your body would have no mechanisms with which to counteract the varying degrees of stress that each day throws at it. What we sometimes interpret as an alarming symptom needing to be quieted at all costs is in fact a welcome indicator that your body has recognised that it needs to prepare itself for challenges ahead.

If your body is successful in its quest for balance, it will have maintained normal levels of internal temperature, pressure and chemistry. However, if the stress facing your body is perceived to be long-standing or extreme, for example, it will kick-start a selection of internal changes known as *general adaptation syndrome* (*GAS*), first described by Hans Seyle.

It is your hypothalamus (which controls the pituitary gland and is in charge of what's known as the 'mind-over-body' phenomenon) that is to blame! When it thinks your survival is in danger through the onset of a stressor (and it may well be right), it initiates the GAS through two sets of responses: the alarm reaction and the resistance reaction. If these responses are unable successfully to fight the stressor, a third stage, that of exhaustion, is reached.

The alarm reaction

The alarm reaction is also known as the fight-or-flight response. This response is short-lived but dramatic, and is an excellent example of the complexity of the human body as well as of the simplicity with which the body perceives the external world.

When the hypothalamus triggers the alarm reaction, high levels of glucose and oxygen are delivered to the brain (you need to be on full alert through stress), the skeletal muscles (as far as your body knows, you may need physically to fight the stressor) and the heart (which must dramatically step up its usual pace to ensure that the brain and muscles have the materials they need).

The adrenal medulla (the inner sections of the adrenal glands) increase their secretion of epinephrine and norepinephrine, otherwise known as adrenaline and noradrenaline. It is these hormones that increase blood pressure, constrict blood vessels, speed up your heart rate and breathing rate, widen your airways, raise blood-sugar levels and decrease your rate of digestion. The overall aim of these responses is to ensure that you have the necessary energy to overcome the stressor. Your body goes through the processes of assessing which organs and body systems will be most useful in its quest for survival. Anything that is not vital to survival, such as digestion and reproduction, is shut down or inhibited.

ABOUT ADRENALINE

The hormones adrenaline and noradrenaline prepare your body for action. They link the nervous and the endocrine systems in providing you with an impressive range of effects in order to fight or flee from the stress that you face. In the short term, these hormones can give us the push we need to get through something (such as making a presentation or performing on stage). However, if our body perceives the need to secrete adrenaline and noradrenaline in the long term, the diseases associated with excessive negative stress, such as a rapid heartbeat and raised blood pressure, are more likely to result.

The resistance reaction

This reaction is far longer-lived than the alarm reaction. During this stage, the hormones that your body releases encourage the conservation of sodium ions. This in turn leads to water retention, which has the knock-on effect of increasing blood volume and therefore maintaining the high blood pressure triggered by the alarm response. But don't be too hard on your body for keeping its fluid levels high – it is only making sure that it can cope with any severe bleeding that it might experience through stress! (Remember, many of the stress responses that we have now are very similar to those our ancestors would have had when confronting savage beasts.)

Other hormones are released by your body during the resistance reaction to keep your body supplied with the energy, proteins and circulatory changes it needs in order to work towards regaining its balance. If it is successful, the stressor is beaten. If it fails despite its continued fighting, then the GAS moves into the stage of exhaustion.

Exhaustion

In the quest to retain sodium ions, your body loses potassium and hydrogen ions in a potentially lethal trade-off. Loss of potassium in your cells means that they function with decreasing effectiveness until they begin to die. Clearly, this stage requires rapid treatment if death is to be avoided. Exhaustion can also be caused by a general weakening of the organs, particularly if the resistance reaction has been prolonged. If your general health is not good, the chances of reaching exhaustion as a result of going though the alarm reaction and the resistance reaction are heightened.

> ## **ABOUT** THE PHYSIOLOGICAL STRESS RESPONSE
>
> The way that the human body responds to what it perceives as a stressor, and therefore a potential threat to life, is pretty impressive. We may bemoan the fact that our blood pressure has risen, or that we are suffering from digestive problems, but these symptoms are all evidence that our body is working to maintain balance. When the body thinks it is in danger it will adapt to the threat. The key is to appreciate this fact and to recognise how our perception of the events that face us in our day-to-day lives has a direct effect on our physical bodies. When your body responds to stress it is trying to save your life!

The effects of stress

Looking at the physiological responses that your body has to the stressors it faces, it is clear that just about every system is affected. But clearly not all stress in our lives leads to a state of exhaustion; and death, as a direct and indisputable result of negative stress and no other factors, is still thought to be relatively uncommon. We do need to retain a perspective on this; in most cases, negative stress will perhaps have a dramatic impact on our life but it won't kill us.

Burnout

Burnout is characterised by loss of interest and motivation typically in people who normally work with commitment and drive. Those who are burned out can be physically, emotionally or psychologically exhausted. The symptoms and warning signs of burnout include:

- a sense of diminishing control over aspects of your life
- an increasing incidence of negative thoughts
- a negative feeling, often misplaced, about what you are achieving each day
- loss of a sense of purpose
- demotivation and disenchantment with work and life
- detachment from life, in particular work and relationships
- headaches and dizziness
- palpitations and chest pain
- sleeplessness and night terrors or nightmares
- loss of concentration
- increased dependency on stimulants or tranquillizers

Suffering burnout does not necessarily mean having to change jobs or leave the profession. What it does mean is taking a sensible look at the way in which you are working and making lasting changes that support your personal well-being. This will invariably involve a period of time off work to revaluate your life and work – which is not, in any way, a bad thing.

ABOUT THE MASLACH BURNOUT INVENTORY

The Maslach Burnout Inventory is thought to be one of the leading measures of burnout in educators. The survey takes about fifteen minutes to complete and addresses three general scales: emotional exhaustion, depersonalisation and personal accomplishment.

Do a search on the Internet to find out more about the Maslach Burnout Inventory.

Take rest; a field that has rested gives a beautiful crop.

(Ovid)

ACTION Are you at risk of burnout at work? Ask yourself these questions. The more you can answer positively the better:

- Are you satisfied in your work? YES/NO
- Do you feel adequately remunerated? YES/NO
- Can you identify other rewards of work? YES/NO
- Are all elements of your personal well-being nurtured at work? YES/NO
- Can you sense a feeling of personal commitment about your work? YES/NO
- Do you feel energy and enthusiasm about what you are doing at work? YES/NO
- Do you feel that your needs are met at work? YES/NO
- Does your job allow you to express your creativity? YES/NO
- If you had to leave your job for any reason, would you be disappointed/ devastated? YES/NO
- Is your personal rate of absenteeism low? YES/NO
- Are headaches, fatigue, palpitations, sleeplessness, irritability, depression, loss of memory, and so on, rare occurrences for you? YES/NO

Although this is a crude test, if you are not able to answer many of these questions positively you could be at risk of moving towards burnout. It would be wise to talk to your chosen healthcare provider about your concerns sooner rather than later. If you would like to talk to someone anonymously and in confidence, and you live in England or Wales, the Teacher Support Line can help: 08000 562 561 and 0800 085 5088 respectively.

There is nothing you cannot do if you keep calm and go forward.
(Whoopi Goldberg)

Serenity is not freedom from the storm, but peace within the storm.
(Anon.)

The eyes experience less stress when they look upon a wider horizon.
(R D Chin)

EXAMPLE BURNED OUT

I know that I have experienced burnout before, although at the time I don't think that label was put on it. I had started to feel a sense of losing control over my work. I'd find myself doing crazy things like planning to complete ten hours' schoolwork on a Sunday or saying to myself if I get up at 5 a.m. I can get that job done. I felt as though my effectiveness was diminishing yet my workload was increasing. I felt totally swamped, engulfed yet strangely detached. When an Ofsted inspection was announced, I knew something was wrong with me because, while the rest of the staff were getting het up and stressed out, I couldn't care less. I was signed off with stress and had about a month off. Burnout was not mentioned, but reading about it I definitely think that's what I experienced. The only good thing about it is that it's not permanent. I did regain my enthusiasm for life and for my job, and in a way I'm very grateful that it happened. I know the warning signs now, and that's more knowledge than any doctor or book could ever give me. I think I'd say to anyone: Watch out, take care but don't despair if it happens to you. There is light at the end of the tunnel.

(Secondary teacher with twelve years' experience)

EXAMPLE BURNOUT FEARS

Is it just me or does everyone fear they will burn out by half-term?

(Primary NQT [Newly Qualified Teacher])

If you want to feel better, you must realise that your thoughts and atti-tudes – not external events – create your feelings.

(David Burns)

Where does the body end and the mind begin? Where does the mind end and the spirit begin?

(B K S Iyengar)

ABOUT PANIC ATTACKS

Panic attacks can be terrifying evidence that negative stress has taken hold. It's thought that one in ten adults have experienced a panic attack at some point in their life, so if it happens to you you're not alone by any means.

Panic attacks occur for no apparent reason (there is no immediate threat to life) yet they are frighteningly real to the sufferer. It's common to experience a sense of impending doom with a panic attack, and to fear that you are going mad or going to die. These feelings are usually accompanied by sweating, palpitations and shortness of breath, all of which signify severe discontent and must be taken seriously.

If you suspect that you have suffered a panic attack, do talk to your healthcare provider about it. These ideas may help should similar symptoms arise:

- Remember that you are not alone. Panic attacks happen to many people, and the symptoms you are experiencing are your body's normal response to a heightened sense of fear.
- In themselves, panic attacks are harmless. You won't die from them, and the sense of impending doom that you may experience does not bring forth disaster. The feelings at the height of an attack are the worst that will happen.
- Repeat an affirmation to yourself often when you sense that panic may be rising. Choose words such as 'balance', 'calm', 'peace' and 'serenity' to focus on and repeat to yourself. Get right into the present moment by focusing on different parts of your body. How do your shoulders feel? Relax them. How does your stomach feel? Relax it. Are your fists clenched? Relax them.
- Stay in the present moment – no 'what ifs'.
- Don't fight it – the panic attack will soon pass.
- Concentrate on your breathing. Slow, deep breaths will help you best.
- Allow yourself to notice the feeling subside. It won't last for ever.

Talk to your chosen healthcare provider after suffering a panic attack. Panic attacks are evidence that underlying dis-ease is gaining a hold, so take action sooner rather than later.

EXAMPLE TUNNEL FEARS

I was approaching a tunnel when I experienced my first panic attack. My father had suffered from them, so I recognised the symptoms, but that didn't help when these overwhelming feelings of impending doom washed over me. I felt as though I was drowning, and I had this incredible fear that I would not be able to drive through the tunnel. I had a bottle of water on the seat beside me, and I took the lid off and literally shook it all over my face to try to shock myself out of it. It was terrifying. I felt that I was going to die, that my death was inevitable if I drove into the tunnel. But somewhere in my mind I knew that I had to do it. I gripped the wheel and fixed my eyes on the number plate of the car in front. I was breathing noisily and fast. When I was over halfway through, the feelings started to subside. I started to know that I wasn't going to die and that I would make it through. Goodness only knows what I looked like! I was soaking wet and staring at the car in front, white knuckles gripped to the wheel! But at the time the feelings are real – more real than any you've ever experienced. The only word for it is *terrifying*.

(Primary teacher with three years' experience)

ACTION When you feel in a state of panic, relax your jaw by unclenching your teeth, placing your lips lightly together and your teeth slightly apart. It is virtually impossible to retain tension in your face in this position. Then start 4-2-4-2 breathing: breathe in to a slow count of four, hold for two, breathe out to a slow count of four, hold for two. Focus closely on your breathing until you feel the panic start to recede.

Breakdown

When negative stress is experienced for a sustained period of time, and no workable solution is found, or attempted to be found, then breakdown can result. This may be triggered by a life crisis, or by the drip, drip effect of disappointment in life, exhaustion, demoralisation and so on.

Breakdown can be both physical and mental/emotional. There are always warning signs, but if these are not perceived, or not acted upon, they eventually become overwhelming until there is no option but to seek appropriate treatment.

Breakdown may not be as dramatic or as sudden as it sounds. It can occur slowly and build up until one day something happens to make normal life impossible to continue. This can manifest itself in a variety of ways, for example, severe depression, hyperactivity, excessive anxiety, self-destructive behaviour such as self-harm or thoughts of suicide, making sudden changes to relationships or walking out of your job. It is essential to seek help from any professional source that seems appropriate to you as soon as you suspect that the process of breakdown may be occurring.

EXAMPLE BREAKDOWN

I honestly didn't see it coming, and even when I was going through it I wasn't fully aware of what was happening, but one day I just couldn't go to school. I wasn't ill, I didn't think I needed to see a doctor, but I couldn't do the usual routine, couldn't pack my bag for school, couldn't even get dressed. It was as if I had ground to a halt. I saw my GP that day, and that was the start of a very long recovery. I was diagnosed with a work-stress-related nervous breakdown, but that label didn't mean much when it came to my recovery. The essence of what happened to me was that my life, as I had been living it, became unworkable. I ignored the warning signs that I had had over the years and papered over my stresses and dissatisfactions. I had to rebuild from the lowest point I have ever been but I am grateful that it happened to me. Does that sound bizarre? I really am pleased that I had the chance to do that. Breaking down was good for me. I fell apart for a while, but I got myself back again and I know myself more now than I ever thought possible. And, yes, I am teaching again, but not in a way I'd ever taught before. I have to come first. Without that attention to myself, I know that I'm nothing in the classroom.

(Secondary teacher with thirteen years' experience)

Recognising the signs of negative stress

We all exhibit certain symptoms when we feel overwhelmed or stressed, yet it can still be very hard to identify, despite the range of behavioural, physical and emotional clues your body may be throwing out. If you think you may be suffering from negative stress, consider these questions:

- What do others say about you? How are you described?
- How do you interact with others? Are you patient and attentive or snappy and distracted?
- Are you less confident than you used to be? Shyer and more introspective?
- Is your mood stable and balanced or do you find yourself swinging from contentment to distress in one go?
- Is decision-making more difficult than it used to be and concentration a thing of the past?
- Are your thoughts generally positive or negative? Do you have any thoughts of impending doom? Are you tearful and depressed?
- Have your sleeping patterns changed? Do you find yourself waking at night, or else constantly tired and falling asleep at the first opportunity?
- Do you rely on stimulants more than usual? Has the occasional drink become a daily necessity? Are you smoking? Or smoking more than usual?
- Have there been changes to your eating habits? Is your appetite as it was?
- Has work taken over where leisure once reigned? Once you have completed your work do you have the energy for a full social life?
- What are your energy levels like? Do you experience the highs and lows of adrenaline 'dependence'?
- Are you constantly fighting low-level infections such as colds and sore throats? Are you suffering from headaches or aches in other parts of your body?
- Do you ever experience palpitations or waves of fear or panic?
- Are you able to distinguish between external and internal pressures?

There are some classic physical symptoms of negative stress. These may not, of course, all occur in the same person, but may be felt at different times depending on the nature of the cause of the negative stress. It's important to be alert to the following as they relate to changes taking place as a result of excessive stress:

In the body:

- the blood supply to the muscles increases
- the adrenal glands produce more adrenaline

- pupils become dilated
- the heart rate increases
- blood pressure can rise
- the sweat glands produce more sweat
- breathing becomes more rapid or troubled, with hyperventilation
- swallowing can become difficult
- muscles can become tense and rigid
- blood-sugar levels can rise
- frequency of urination increases
- frequency of headaches and migraine can increase
- the menstrual cycle can become disturbed
- the digestive system can become upset; nausea can result
- the immune system becomes less effective
- fatigue and exhaustion can develop
- skin problems can develop such as dryness, rashes, blushing and acne
- speech can slow
- fatigue can develop
- the face can flush or look pale

In the mind:

- anxiety and nervousness can develop
- depression and moodiness can arise
- feelings of loneliness and isolation can develop
- emotional outbursts or uncharacteristic behaviour may occur
- concentration and decision-making can become difficult
- sensitivity to others can increase, particularly concerning perceived criticism
- excessive self-criticism can occur
- situation avoidance can develop
- the desire for inactivity or excessive activity may arise
- over-dependence on stimulants or addictive behaviour may result

This is by no means an exhaustive list, but it does highlight the extent of the impact that negative stress can have on us. This is not something to ignore.

ABOUT WARNING SIGNS

Many believe that the body gives warning signs of increasing urgency. Although it may well be whispering its discontent at first, if you don't listen it may end up shouting. Don't ignore it until you're deafened by its pleas for attention. If a stressor leads to symptoms of negative stress as your body responds to the situation it faces, your condition will deteriorate if you don't modify your behaviour. Symptoms are likely to be physical, then emotional and then mental.

We even know that certain diseases are known to be caused, at least in part, by negative stress. Conditions such as eczema, asthma, hypertension, peptic ulcers and irritable bowel syndrome all have clear links to negative stress. It is even thought to contribute to conditions such as cancer and rheumatoid arthritis, and some healthcare providers will go as far as saying that any condition or symptom felt either physically or emotionally may have a root in negative stress.

ABOUT THE LINE BETWEEN CHALLENGE AND NEGATIVE STRESS

There's a fine line between challenge and negative stress, sometimes so fine that it's barely perceptible. It takes sophisticated self-knowledge to enable us to see precisely where we have drawn it at any one time as its location will move depending on a variety of external and internal factors. The sooner we can appreciate this, and learn how to use this information to our advantage, the sooner we will be free from the effects of negative stress.

ABOUT POST-TRAUMATIC STRESS DISORDER

Post-traumatic Stress Disorder, or PTSD as it is known, is thought to affect 1 per cent of the general population at any time. It has been clinically defined as 'the development of characteristic symptoms following a psychologically distressing event outside the range of normal human experience', and is recognised as a separate category of anxiety disorder.

According to Simon Meyerson, a consultant psychologist and expert in PTSD, the condition is caused by 'a psychological blast to the mind'. In his experience, it is the personality and not the physical body that begins to crumble.

PTSD is relatively uncommon in those who have suffered traumas that did not threaten their lives. It is always diagnosed in connection with a known and identifiable cause.

Characteristic symptoms of PTSD include hopelessness, depression, compulsions, violence, preoccupation, chronic fatigue, self-neglect and phobic responses.

Stress and well-being

We may be aware of what well-being means as a concept, and of what positive and negative stress can do for us, but there is an extent to which our response to external and internal pressures needs to acknowledge that, even though positive stress and negative stress are evidently different, they are both still *stress*.

Some writers on stress and the impact that it can have on our lives have referred to negative stress as having a toxic effect on our body. Taken to its conclusion, this belief would suggest that we need to detoxify if we know we are experiencing negative stress and are seeking to rebalance ourselves.

Sources of stress

We only need to consider the range of sources of stress in our lives to be able to see just how comprehensively our sense of personal well-being can be affected. It's not just what happens at work and in the classroom, but everything else in the wider experience of life that can serve to stress us.

In 1967 researchers Holmes and Rahe studied the relative impact of life events on stress-related symptoms (Table 2.1). The scale they devised assigns values, based on the sample of 394 individuals being told that marriage represents 50 points, to common life events. The values are intended to show the comparison between stressors and are not intended to be added together. You may well be able to add events of your own to the list.

The Holmes and Rahe 'Social Readjustment Rating Scale' appeared in the *Journal of Psychosomatic Research II* (pp. 213–218) in 1967.

Table 2.1

Events	Scale of impact
Death of spouse	100
Divorce	75
Marital separation	65
Jail term	63
Death of a close family member	63
Personal injury or illness	53
Marriage	50
Dismissal from work	47
Marital reconciliation	45
Retirement	45
Change in health of family member	44
Pregnancy	40
Sex difficulties	39
Gain of new family member	39
Business readjustment	39
Change in financial state	38
Death of close friend	37
Change to different line of work	36
Change in number of arguments with spouse	36
Major mortgage	31
Foreclosure of mortgage or loan	30
Change in responsibilities at work	29
Son or daughter leaving home	29
Trouble with in-laws	29
Outstanding personal achievement	28
Partner begins or stops work	26
Begin or end school	26
Change in living conditions	25

continued on next page

Revision of personal habits	24
Trouble with boss	23
Change in work hours or conditions	20
Change in residence/school/recreation	19
Change in social activities	18
Small mortgage or loan	17
Change in sleeping/eating habits	16
Change in number of family get-togethers	15
Vacation	13
Christmas	12
Minor violations of the law	11

ACTION What would you add to the Holmes–Rahe Social Adjustment Scale?

What values would you assign to these events?

Would you say that these are positive or negative events?

Are you surprised that so-called positive events can still exert stress on you?

The mind can only reflect the true image of the Self when it is tranquil and wholly relaxed.

(*Indira Gandhi*)

The human body is the best picture of the human soul.

(*Ludwig Wittgenstein*)

For every time in stress, you need a recovering time in relaxation.

(*Emmett E Miller, MD*)

ABOUT STRESS AND PERSONALITY

It may seem an over-simplification, but fundamentally we have an in-built mechanism that perceives everything in our external world as a potential threat. Call it a quirk of survival, but it certainly kick-starts the body into a state of fight or flight. But the speed of this response, some say, is dependent upon our personality type.

Type A people are reportedly ambitious workaholics. They are perfectionists, too, and find it difficult to relax and switch off. There's a passion about the way in which they live their life, but this can lead to an emotional crash should anything significantly hinder their progress and achievement. Heart attacks are relatively common amongst this group.

Type B people are supposedly more laid back. They live with less of the intensity of type As, and are not as comfortable with deadlines and pressure. Perhaps not surprisingly, there are fewer heart attacks among this group.

Type T people are the risk-takers. A relatively newly identified group, these appear to thrive on stress and actively seek risky situations such as taking part in extreme sports.

Most people could legitimately claim to be a mixture of type A, type B and type T, and a balance between the three would certainly seem to be most sustainable. Is that how you would describe yourself or do you sit more comfortably in one type or another?

The important thing to remember about stress and personality types is that one group is not necessarily more negatively stressed than another. One of the most crucial factors that experience of stress depends on is our sense of *control*.

There is evidence to suggest that stress is in the *person* and not in the *position*. Many jobs are apparently stressful, but they are not experienced as such by all who do them. It is well worth considering where you perceive stress to be in your life; inherent in your job, or a dimension of you the person?

EXAMPLE COP-OUTS

To say that teaching is a stressful job is a cop-out and avoids the situation in education where as soon as a teacher gets really good at the job they are removed to an alternative profession of people management for which they – in some cases – have not received adequate training and which, for a variety of reasons, can cause stress in them and others. The skills are completely different, and the transition is not always smooth.

(Educationalist)

ACTION
Are you addicted to the drive that stress gives you? Some people are. Ask yourself these questions. If you answer yes to most of them, you just might be . . .

- After achieving something challenging or meeting a tight deadline do you feel high? YES/NO
- Do you ever leave things right to the last minute? YES/NO
- Do you think that you can only achieve to a high standard when under pressure? YES/NO
- Do you say yes to additional workload more often than you say no? YES/NO
- Do you create challenges through not pacing yourself? YES/NO
- Do you feel better about yourself when you can say that each day is packed with teaching, meetings and planning, etc.? Does it affect your self-esteem? YES/NO

Responding to perceived stress

At any one time, the way in which you respond to perceived stress is dependent on a number of variable factors:

- personality
- personal circumstances (for example, your marital status, finances, relationships, work pressures, and so on)
- experience of life so far
- diet and fitness levels

- your ability to recognise symptoms
- self-esteem
- ability to relax
- skills of organisation

If you remember one thing from this chapter, it should be that nothing to do with stress is set in stone. Your response to a stressor one week may be far more dramatic than in another week. That's because your body and mind are essentially responding to each perceived threat with the tools and know-how they have *at the time*. A little self-understanding in this respect will go a long way in helping to neutralise the impact of any negative stress.

ACTION Do you have a stress-resistant personality?

Studies have shown that, even though some people may experience high levels of stress in their lives, they are still able to resist being overwhelmed by its ill-effects. It is thought that this is because they have the following three characteristics:

- Control – over their purpose and direction in life
- Challenge – seeing change as a positive aspect of life
- Commitment – to the various dimensions of life, e.g. work, family, friends, hobbies and so on.

Do you think that you possess these naturally? Have you had to learn to possess them? Or do you consider that you are yet to develop them?

CHAPTER 3

Well-being and stress in teaching – the obvious causes

I am a teacher at heart, and there are moments in the classroom when I can hardly hold the joy. When my students and I discover uncharted territory to explore, when the pathway out of a thicket opens up before us, when our experience is illuminated by the lightning-life of the mind – then teaching is the finest work I know.

But at other moments, the classroom is so lifeless or painful or confused – and I am so powerless to do anything about it – that my claim to be a teacher seems a transparent sham. Then, the enemy is everywhere: in those students from some alien planet, in that subject I thought I knew, and in the personal pathology that keeps me earning my living in this way. What a fool I was to imagine that I had mastered this occult art – harder to divine than tea leaves and impossible for mortals to do even passably well!

(Parker J Palmer, *The Courage to Teach*, page 1)

It is somewhat surprising that so much is currently made of the fact that teaching is often experienced as a 'stressful profession'. When the actual job is considered – what each teacher has to do every day, the sheer number of people with whom they must communicate, what they are held accountable for, and the amount that the job encroaches on personal life – is it any surprise? There are some aspects of the job that are simply unavoidably stressful; but, then, we know that, don't we?

Perhaps the real news story here is that teaching *continues* to be experienced by some as stressful. Long after we have identified what it is about the job that leads to negative stress, these are still issues that are having to be tackled (or not) by schools. And it certainly isn't just weak or struggling teachers that are affected by the demands of the job. Many extremely competent teachers find the juggling act of chores and tasks beyond the classroom too difficult to reconcile with their own personal sense of well-being.

EXAMPLE   A DIFFICULT CHOICE

I wouldn't say I was ever a weak teacher. Nothing in any performance management, appraisal or inspection ever indicated that. But when I started having to devote every waking moment to the job I knew something was wrong. The real decision for me was whether to stay in the profession but change schools or leave altogether. I chose to leave, on the assumption that I could always return if I wanted to (and could get a job). But I still had people say to me that they didn't blame me for not being able to handle the stress. But I did! I left! I made a conscious decision and left. And it was the best thing I could have done at the time because now I am back in the classroom, in a different school and with a more positive attitude. The level of stress I felt has since served as an indicator – I know what I can take now and what tips me over into bad stress. That's an incredibly valuable life lesson.

(Primary teacher with twenty years' experience)

When tackling any negative stress that you feel, remember that small, incremental changes are likely, in most cases, to have the greatest long-term effect. Do also keep in mind that you have a responsibility to take steps to safeguard your health. Only you can know when you have reached your limit of tolerance, and only you will know the stages through which you travel in order to reach this limit. Disempower negative stress by facing, not avoiding, your stressors.

ABOUT AGE

Research findings from the UK, USA, Canada, the Netherlands, Singapore and Finland all point to age as being a determining factor in a teacher's experience of workplace stress. Apparently, older teachers, aged 45 or over, have been found to be more susceptible to negative stress and its related symptoms. With some countries experiencing an ageing teaching population, this may go some way towards explaining why requests for help with workplace stress through, for example, teachers' professional associations have risen, in some cases, alarmingly.

Another factor which may be contributing to this is the amount of energy that the job now requires. Perhaps it is in the process of becoming a 'young person's game'.

Obvious causes of negative stress in the teaching profession

Callers to Teacher Support Line in the UK repeatedly raise a number of issues that are inherently stressful in the job of teaching. These include:

- poor workplace environments
- excessive working time and workload
- lack of personal fulfilment and career prospects
- internal politics and conflict with colleagues
- excessive bureaucracy
- poor communication
- low morale
- resistance to change or excessive change
- a blame culture

These are common themes to be experienced by many teachers worldwide. During the process of research for this book, key causes of negative stress in the profession were raised repeatedly. They coincided strongly with the findings from Teacher Support Line and are dealt with throughout the rest of this book.

Workload

A common perception is that negative stress in teaching centres on the sheer volume of work that teachers must get through. It's as if well-being begins and ends with workload. But that is far from the reality. Of course, workload is an important contributor; but it is not the whole story, and to give it an inflated importance fails to respect the fact that there are factors associated with the job that can have both a negative and a positive impact on your sense of well-being.

Quick pointers

When thinking about the workload facing you, consider these points:

- There is only so much that anyone can achieve in any twenty-four hours. To a certain extent you will need to develop the attitude that you will work as efficiently and effectively as you can, but only within the bounds of reasonable expectation.
- Each twenty-four-hour period (on a workday at least) should provide you with time to work, eat, relax, exercise and sleep. Without a balance between these your efficiency will suffer. Cutting back on everything but work will ultimately prove to be a costly decision in terms of your overall well-being.

It ain't no disgrace for a man to fall, but to lie there and grunt is.
(*Josh Billings*)

Our real blessings often appear to us in the shape of pains, losses and disappointments; but let us have patience, and we soon shall see them in their proper figures.
(*Joseph Addison*)

Worry does not empty tomorrow of its sorrow; it empties today of its strength.
(*Corrie Ten Boom*)

ABOUT DOING A 'TIME AUDIT'

A 'time audit' can help you to see if you are spending lengthy amounts of time on tasks that produce little in the way of a positive outcome for you. Over two or three days, make a note of how you spend your time on an hour-by-hour basis. It is likely that you'll discover at least one point in the day at which time is leaking, whether that be in your school life, home life or the transition between the two. You can plug this leak by placing a limit on how long you devote to a particular activity, or by stopping the activity altogether. For example, if you routinely find you queue to use the photocopier at crucial points in the day (before the start of the first session or during the dinner break), make a point of noticing when the machines are free and use them at these times as much as possible if the queuing is a frustration. This may seem obvious, but relatively minor tweaks in the times that you do things and the ways in which you do them can help you to regain valuable moments.

When doing your time audit, make sure you cover your entire waking day and look at 'home' activities as well as work activities. Is there anything that surprises you about the results? Aim to determine at least one change that you can implement with immediate effect.

Administration

There's an inherent tension between the proper job of educating youngsters in the classroom (actual teaching) and the vast array of peripheral tasks that have to be done. Administration and paperwork, often part of the accountability process, is a major force in many schools worldwide; and this, combined with the role conflict that teachers can sometimes experience, is draining of time and energy.

EXAMPLE A SMALL DEPARTMENT

I'm head of a department of two and a half which is actually hopeless. There's far more work than we can comfortably manage, and I end up having to plead for additional non-contact time just to get through paperwork. I'd far rather be teaching.

(Secondary teacher with four years' experience)

Anecdotal evidence suggests that this situation has worsened in recent years and, while some countries like the UK are seeking to take steps to reduce the administrative burden of teaching, there is still much progress yet to be made.

ACTION Make a list of all the administrative tasks that you have to do. Where do you perceive the greatest leak of time to be? Is there a way of reducing this by working collaboratively? Or not doing the task at all? What is *essential* and what is *desirable*? Is there any chance of taking a break from the desirable to concentrate on the essential?

Quick pointers

- Allocate time during each school week for administrative tasks. Never leave major chores like report-writing until the last minute. Little and often will be a less stressful approach.
- If you have a relative 'slack' time, offer to help a colleague out. The favour will almost certainly be returned.
- Aim to pace yourself through predictably busy times.

The home–work interface

There isn't a teacher anywhere who doesn't take their work home. If this isn't literally in the form of marking, planning and assessment, it's in the form of mentally replaying scenes from the day, going over interactions with pupils and preparing for the challenges of the day ahead.

For those teachers who live with a partner, the potential for tension here is increased, especially if both work. The sheer overload of trying to cope with a teaching life and a home life can be incredibly demanding, and interpersonal conflicts between the various members of a family unit can occur.

Happiness is produced not so much by great pieces of good fortune that seldom happen as by little advantages that occur every day.

(Benjamin Franklin)

Quick pointers

These ideas may help:

- Managing these two major dimensions of your life requires finely honed skills, many of which are explored in depth in this book. In the short term, though, the most effective way of not blurring the home–work interface too drastically is to devise clear ways of cutting off between the two.
- Complete as much work in the school building as you can. Minimise what you take home.
- Have at least one full day off every weekend and at least one night off every week.
- Make 'dates' with the people you live with to spend quality time together.
- Contain your schoolwork when it's at home. Don't allow it to spread through every room of the house.

EXAMPLE   HOME WORKING

I can tell you exactly what would improve the quality of my working life, and that would be having a home life! I can't remember the last time my wife and I actually sat down together to talk. I feel like I don't know her any more. There's something very wrong when it's not possible to get your working day completed in a reasonable number of hours. What if I just said, 'No, I can't mark these books, because I'm going to go home and relax, spend some time with my wife and kids and watch a bit of TV'? People do that, don't they?

(Secondary teacher with fifteen years' experience)

Locus of control

The notion of negative stress emerging purely from having too much to do is not a useful one. In fact, it's pretty nonsensical. But what is responsible to a great extent is the degree of control we perceive that we have over our work and our life in general. As the serenity prayer says, we need the wisdom to know the difference between what we *can* change and what we *cannot* change.

Whether we see ourselves as agents or as victims of control in our lives is central to our ability to maintain a sense of well-being. Research has shown that those who feel an internal locus of control are more able to cope when stressors are imposed from outside them than those who have an external locus of control.

For those with an internal locus of control, the workplace is by definition a less hostile and stressful place to be than it is for those with an external locus of control. Interestingly, depressive people tend to have an external locus of control.

This is particularly interesting when translated into the school as a place of work. While being a teacher in a classroom is a pretty autonomous way to spend your career, many teachers perceive that this control is not complete, mostly because of the prescriptive nature of some school curricula, the extent of inspection that schools undergo and the lack of resources that some schools experience. The outcome for the teacher can be a strange dichotomy.

ACTION You have direct control over many things in life, not least your thoughts and whether you adopt a positive, optimistic attitude or a negative, pessimistic attitude.

What's it to be? What's your choice?

Quick pointers

When considering the issue of control in your working life, these ideas may help:

- Identify what autonomy you do have at work. Precisely what aspects do you have control over? When you start to list them you will be surprised at how many there are.
- Aim to identify if the school management you work under likes to empower teachers with a sense of control or retain control for themselves. How much freedom do you have in your work? How 'consulted' do you feel about both major and minor decisions?
- Where do you feel restricted at work? Consider discussing this with your line manager and build these talks around your need to shift the locus of control, even if subtly, so that it is more in your favour.

EXAMPLE SHARING CONTROL

My current head is the best one I've ever worked with. She is very good at telling us about decisions she's having to make for the school and at gathering our opinions. Sometimes she'll say: Look, I had to go ahead with this even though I know it's not popular but I really didn't see a way round it. And we believe her because most of the time our opinions are sought. That's all it takes – just a little bit of consultation. It makes the biggest difference, I think.

(Primary teacher with seven years' experience)

Accountability and inspection

Accountability is a central theme running through teachers' professional lives yet this is somehow at odds with the nature of the job. While no teacher worthy of the title would deny the need for accountability, it is important to recognise that it is essentially a professional, quantitative agenda. Teachers could be considered to be creatives who are expected to account for themselves as if they were a very different kind of professional.

To whom and to what teachers are accountable cannot easily be answered. It would seem that teachers must follow the steps of a complex dance, the tune to which may be provided by their school managers, the governing body, the local authority, parents, pupils, inspectors, society, governments, and so on. This should be a tune of beautiful harmony, but occasionally what results is a cacophony.

The fact that accountability is a necessary part of professional life is not in question. Teachers know that they have a duty to reach exacting national standards. But knowing who you, as a teacher, are accountable to is often more problematic. Accountability appears to have a symbolic meaning separate from its literal meaning, and this symbolism can strike fear at the heart of even the most conscientious of teachers. In fact, it is often such teachers that suffer most at the hands of their own self-doubt and self-criticism, seeing accountability either as a regulatory mechanism or as something that needs to be externally applied in order for them to perform their duties to acceptable standards. However, accountability should not force you to define your practice defensively; if anything, it should encourage a positive response in providing clarity and transparency in your work to all those you are working for.

For the purposes of any formal system of inspection such as Ofsted inspection in England, it is wise not to focus on the wider (public) picture of accountability. Simply follow the guidance of your managers and leaders, and think no further than your immediate accountability (with pupils in mind) to your headteacher and governors. When your school is undergoing an inspection, your accountability does not change. Inspectors do not assume a place in the hierarchy of your school's management, and so within your school you remain accountable to those that you work with.

Quick pointers

To help you to maintain your well-being when facing an inspection, consider these ideas:

- Some self-help remedies have an established record of benefit. Bach Rescue Remedy is great for quick results. Either put four drops directly on your tongue, or into a small quantity of water which can be sipped at regular intervals. You can now buy Rescue Remedy in a spray dispenser, too.
- The homeopathic remedy *Argentum Nitricum* has a great track record for those who feel they are suffering from internal turmoil. Low potencies are available from high-street pharmacies, but it is usually best to visit a qualified practitioner so that you take the potency most suited to you.
- Remember to eat little and often. This will help you maintain healthy blood-sugar levels. If these fluctuate too wildly, you may feel more stressed than you really are.
- Book a stress-busting treatment (such as a massage) early in your inspection week. Do not feel that you cannot afford the time – an hour of pure relaxation is sure to increase your productivity in the long run.
- Talk to colleagues about their experiences. They may be able to offer you some valuable perspectives. You may even realise that you are coping better than anyone else!
- Utilise your school's support systems (many headteachers now set aside time during inspections in which to listen to the concerns and stresses of staff members).

- Try not to attach yourself to a particular outcome. The inspection has arrived, and what will be will be. Trust that the judgements made will be accurate, and remember that if you feel this is not the case there are steps you can take to make your feelings known. Inspection does not have to threaten your health and well-being – it's only a temporary situation.
- Do not forget to breathe; not the way you usually breathe, but taking slow, deep breaths that allow you physically to relax.
- Be prepared for changes taking place as a result of any inspection process that your school goes through, even if the result is overwhelmingly positive. It's worth noting that, while this change may bring progress and improvement, it can also be unsettling and demanding, as adjustments must be made.

Quantity of interpersonal contacts

In a book about well-being it's probably not a wise idea to state that teachers, typically, are involved in around a thousand interpersonal contacts every day. Whether this is just a brief word in the corridor or a sustained conversation with a pupil or colleague, whether reactive or proactive, predictable or unpredictable, confrontational or amicable, these interactions take place, and teachers must be mentally fit enough to adapt their persona as appropriate in every situation as and when necessary. It's not easy, even for those who insist that they are a 'people person'.

Quick pointers

If you find the quantity of interpersonal contacts you make each day burdensome on occasion, these ideas may help:

- Make sure that you can have a part of each day alone, with no people or voices from music or radio. Even if you can only achieve five minutes or so of silence, perhaps in the car on the way to work, or in the shower or bath, this will give your brain temporary respite from having to think about what it's hearing and formulate a mental or spoken response.
- Consider joining a meditation or relaxation group that has a built-in period of silence as part of its practice.

- Limit your communication with others. Don't get into lengthy discussions when a short conversation will do.
- Become mindful of the times in your day when you don't have to talk to other people, for example, when using the bathroom.

EXAMPLE CRAVING PEACE

I sometimes get totally overwhelmed at school by the noise and chatter everywhere you turn. When it starts to get to me it *really* gets to me. I have even sat in the staffroom with the phone to my ear pretending to be on the phone so that I don't have to talk to anyone! If I want to be alone at school, I have to walk round the playground; but then kids inevitably come up and want to talk. I really think this is something that schools need to address. We may love working with young people, but some of us need at least one quiet break in the day.

(Primary NQT)

Behaviour and indiscipline

If you are a teacher, try not to merely transmit knowledge, but try at the same time to awaken your students' minds to basic human qualities such as kindness, compassion, forgiveness and understanding. Do not communicate these as though they were the reserve of ethics or religion. Show them that these qualities are indispensable for the happiness and survival of everyone.

(His Holiness the Dalai Lama)

The persistent and consistent poor behaviour that many teachers find themselves dealing with is evidence of the disconnectedness of many pupils from the environment in which they find themselves. Reconnecting pupils to the educational system through which they must travel is a colossal task and one which will not, and cannot, be achieved in the long term through behaviour-management tips. Yet the fact remains that one of the biggest obstacles to widespread well-being among teachers in schools is the behaviour of the students in their classes.

Battling the consequences of low motivation, poor social skills, boredom, disenfranchisement and belligerence cannot be achieved alone. It has to be done at every level of the school's community and the wider forum of society in general. When pupils sometimes break the rules with full knowledge of the consequences, it's no surprise that when teachers face conflict with children their emotional undercarriage opens and energy drops out in an instant. This is as sure a recipe for negative stress in schools as anything.

Quick pointers

Consider these if behaviour issues are a source of concern:

- You are not, and cannot be, solely responsible for any poor behaviour or blatant indiscipline exhibited in your classroom. The cause of this will, at best, be due to a variety of factors.
- Poor and challenging behaviour in the classroom is almost never aimed directly *at* the teacher. It is *not* a personal thing. It emerges from an inability in the child appropriately to express anger, often combined with a shuddering lack of self-respect.
- Techniques that you employ to encourage pupils to behave in a manner conducive to learning will have a positive effect to some degree all of the time. Sometimes these techniques will have an astounding effect, and the progress you make will be stunning. At other times, the spectre that is Child From Hell will succeed in destroying most of the attempts you make at creating unity in the classroom. Your personal value as a teacher remains the same; it's just outer circumstances that move beyond our control at times.
- Don't be timid about setting boundaries. It's what your pupils want and need.

ACTION How do children gain your attention in your lessons? Is this through positive behaviour or negative? Are you a reactive teacher, responding to what you see going on, or proactive, pre-empting indiscipline with ease?

- Always, always give your classes behaviour choices. Your goal is not power *over* your students but power *with* them. You are working together as a team.

- Never press on with a lesson when it would be better to stop and discuss your relationships and the way things are going for you all. Be yourself, be authentic; this will reduce the level of negative stress that you feel.
- At the earliest possible opportunity, seek guidance with classes that present behaviour issues for you. There will be structures within your school to deal with this, and your immediate line manager can tell you what support is available to you.

EXAMPLE FINDING A PERSPECTIVE

The biggest lesson for me so far (and I hate to admit that it took me over five years to realise this) was that when a lesson goes what I call 'bad' it's not the whole class that's involved. Often I can narrow it down to just one or two individuals. The second-biggest lesson was not to become so obsessed about the one or two that messed around that I lost sight of the remaining twenty-eight that do actually want to learn. I do what I can outside the classroom to get to know these kids but I am absolutely adamant that they will not ruin my lessons for the bulk of the class. The worst thing I can do for me and my other pupils is pander to them. The one good thing about characters like this is the diversity they bring.

(Secondary teacher with six years' experience)

EXAMPLE GETTING OUT

Behaviour finally got to me. I've had enough. My classes either refuse to work or won't shut up. I'm on sick leave taking Valium and have resigned. They've won. I'm not a zoo keeper.

(Secondary teacher with two years' experience)

Physical working environment

How would you describe your working environment? Too often, teachers around the world feel that they are working in schools that are poorly designed for their current use. Classrooms are frequently described as being too small and inappropriate for mixed-ability classes where anything other than rote learning in rigid rows may be taking place.

Teachers can find themselves having to share crucial resources such as classrooms and teaching space, struggling with no adequate space to organise their tools of the trade, having to function under inadequate lighting and cramming books in piles on the floor rather than on purpose-built shelves. Does this sound anything like your experience?

Of course this isn't the case in every school in all countries, but it certainly can be the experience for some teachers. And it's not simply the environment in which teachers and students work that can affect well-being. The implications for behaviour and achievement all need to be considered, too.

EXAMPLE SPACE TO TEACH

I often wondered what I might be able to achieve with my kids if I had a suitable room to teach them in. I don't need fancy resources, just enough physical space, decent furniture and the opportunity to adapt my teaching space for the different strategies I'd like to employ. Instead we all too often feel cramped and tetchy with each other. I know that this affects achievement levels but what can I do?

(Primary teacher with five years' experience)

Quick pointers

Consider these ideas:

- You may not be able to make substantial changes to the area in which you work, but you can maximise its potential. Make sure it's clean and tidy for a start. Although cleanliness isn't necessarily down to you (talk to your headteacher or premises manager if there are cleaning issues), tidiness is.
- Introduce something of nature such as a plant or some flowers. Involve the pupils in caring for them.
- Make sure the walls look cared for. Keep displays up to date or at least 'current' and fill any blank spaces as appropriate with pictures of calm-

ing scenes. You don't want a cluttered look, but a blank canvas isn't exactly inspiring.

ABOUT INDOOR AIR QUALITY

There is a relationship between indoor air quality and the health and well-being of students and teachers. It is thought that levels of pollutants inside can be anything up to a hundred times higher than outdoor levels.

Many factors such as radon, dust, mildew, mould and carbon monoxide among others affect indoor air quality. Dampness in particular is thought to contribute to respiratory symptoms such as asthma and allergies. In the USA alone, asthma is responsible for 14 million missed schooldays per year.

Indoor air quality does not receive the focus in the UK that it does in the USA and elsewhere. That said, teachers everywhere can take these steps to ensure that the air quality in their classrooms is as good as it can be:

- Raise the issue of indoor air quality as often as you can through the proper channels in your school. The higher a profile air quality has in your school, the more likely it is that action will be taken to improve it.
- Make sure spills are cleaned as quickly as possible to avoid mould growing.
- Check that your classroom is cleaned to a high standard every day and in particular that it is dusted.
- Keep an eye out for pests and report any you find through the proper channels in your school.
- Aim to avoid keeping animals in your classroom. If you do have any, make sure that their cages are scrupulously clean all the time and that animal feed is stored in a sealed container.
- Ensure that rubbish is removed from your workspace on a daily basis.
- Do not store food in your workspace.
- Watch out for condensation on the windows and water-pipes. This should be reported if it occurs in your workspace.
- Check that there are no leaks in your classroom.
- Make sure that your classroom has proper ventilation. The windows should be in full working order, and air should be able to flow freely around the room.
- Report any odours through the proper channels in your school.
- Consider putting a pot plant in your classroom to help convert the carbon dioxide, created by having thirty or so people in one room, back into oxygen.

- If you have particular needs in your room or workspace, such as broken blinds and furniture, windows that don't open, cramped conditions and so on, raise these concerns through the appropriate channels as often as possible. Use your skills of assertiveness to put your case forward and wait to see if your needs are heard. A member of your school's governing body may be able to apply some pressure. Quite significant changes can sometimes come from relatively little expenditure, but concerns must first be raised.
- Organise resources for ease of use and aim to blitz these once a year in an annual spring-clean.

ACTION Think about what your ideal classroom would look like. If money was no object, what would you have in it? How would you arrange it? Make a list and then go through it to see if there is anything you can do to implement change immediately. Just a few small tweaks could enhance your workspace no end.

Workplace bullying

It is a sad and ironic fact that of those who contact the workplace bullying website, www.bullyonline.org, teachers form the largest occupational group. And there is a mountain of anecdotal evidence to suggest that this is reflected elsewhere on national and international support and advice lines regarding bullying in the workplace.

Schools, it seems, are inextricably linked with the concept of bullying, be it between pupils, between pupils and staff or between staff members. While all schools will now have a clear policy on how they seek to tackle bullying between pupils, it is only in recent years that specific policies on handling bullying between adults in the school community have been developed. Historically, it has taken considerable time for staffroom bullying to be identified and dealt with.

Although it seems that schools can be hostile places for some teachers, having the inevitably negative impact on personal and professional well-being, being forewarned about what workplace bullying is and how it can have an impact is being forearmed. The link between suffering as a victim of bullying and experiencing negative stress and even physical illness is indisputable.

A recent survey by a UK teachers' professional association found that almost 40 per cent of respondents felt that their department or faculty head was responsible for the bullying they experienced, and in over half of the reported cases the headteacher was identified as the perpetrator. Bullying of staff seems to take place equally in primary and secondary schools, although, in the UK at least, it is 50 per cent more common in the maintained (or state) sector than it is in the private sector.

ABOUT ADULT BULLIES

An adult bully aims to exert power negatively and consistently over another person with the purpose of inciting fear and causing professional and emotional damage. The bully is inherently destructive, but his/her actions could result from feelings of inadequacy, which have been deflected on to another person, who may be accused of the very flaws the bully detects in himself or herself.

EXAMPLE RECOGNISING BULLYING

I almost cringe when I think of how long it took me to realise what was going on in my school. I was the victim of a workplace bully, and I can see now that time has passed that it went on for ages. The thing that hurt me most about the whole experience was the effect it had on my personality. I really changed during that period. I lost my sense of humour, became nervous and edgy, and ended up questioning just about everything I'd always taken as a truth about myself. I'll never know why I doubted myself more than I doubted my bully, but I know I'll never let it happen again.

(Secondary teacher with ten years' experience)

Believe in yourself! Have faith in your abilities! Without a humble but reasonable confidence in your own powers you cannot be successful or happy.

(Norman Vincent Peale)

ABOUT PERSONALITY CLASHES

Personality clashes are almost inevitable, especially in large schools with huge numbers of staff. It could be that the person you are having difficulties with is someone that other members of staff find hard to relate to as well. Some surreptitious observation will help you here if you suspect that you may be clashing with a colleague.

Never write off a relationship as being beyond hope. It may be stretching your skills of compassion, but there is always a thread of empathy that can be built on. You don't always have to agree with the opinions of others, but you can try to understand why they hold their opinions and why they behave as they do. You may find that those with whom you initially clashed become your closest allies.

Quick pointers

If you're experiencing what you suspect may be workplace bullying, try these ideas:

- Talk to a trusted friend to gain a perspective.
- Reread your job description.
- Attend an assertiveness course or read about assertiveness.
- Seek advice from your union.
- Read your school's policy on workplace bullying.
- Read about workplace bullying.
- Talk to colleagues to gather support.
- Document all communication with your bully.
- Refute all unfair claims made against you.
- Monitor changes in your work performance.
- Visit your healthcare provider.
- Never 'slide out gracefully' against your will.

Powerlessness

A complaint from teachers that was often heard during the research for this book is that a sense of powerlessness can arise from having little, if any, influence on decisions that are made that directly affect the job. This is not peculiar to the teaching profession by any means, and these feelings can be minimised by sensitive leadership.

Quick pointers

If you find yourself battling with powerlessness, consider these points:

- While your opinion may not always be acted upon, your voice can be heard. Whether this is at national level (through elections of policy-makers) or at local level in your community or school, there are channels that exist to ensure that teachers feel consulted. This goes a long way to reduce a sense of powerlessness.
- Become involved in the decision-making process. Take part in official consultations whenever you can and consider becoming a school governor.

ACTION Spend a little time browsing your government's education department website. What opportunities are there for you to give feed-back? What issues would you choose to give feedback on? Resolve to do this in the near future, if not right now.

- If a decision is having an adverse effect on you, keep a record of exactly why this is and make realistic suggestions as to how things could be improved. Make these known through the usual channels in your school. If there is no obvious method of communication, ask for an appointment with the head or other member of your school's senior management team to discuss the matter. No one can guarantee that this approach will solve everything, but the very fact that you have communicated your views will take the edge off any powerlessness you may be feeling.

It is our perceptions, both of ourselves and of each other, including all the diversity of peoples around us, that define who we are and what we are. We are what we believe.

(Lillian Too)

EXAMPLE GETTING INVOLVED

It drives me mad when teachers say that everything is imposed on them. It's actually an apathetic response. We do have a voice and we have strong, influential teaching associations in the UK. We're also frequently asked to consult on policy decisions. I truly believe it's worse in other professions. The thing is that lack of time puts people off getting involved, and I suppose you could argue that that means that we don't *actually* have the chance to get involved, but we shouldn't paint a picture bleaker than the view.

(Secondary teacher with twenty years' experience)

The information age

If you're adept at making computers reduce your workload rather than dramatically add to it, you may not be able to see how the information age could possibly be anything but a boon for teachers. But, for some, techno-stress is a daily reality. From technological difficulties such as unstable software, repeated computer crashes and unreliable access to a machine to the sheer amount of information currently available to teachers right now via the Internet and email, what could help may clearly also intimidate and hinder.

Quick pointers

If the stress of the information age is an issue for you, these ideas may help:

- Although the ground is always shifting when it comes to computer technology, be realistic about what you need to know. Learn the absolute minimum and build on that knowledge at a steady pace.
- Utilise the skills of those around you. It's not just the Information and Communications Technology department in a school that will have technological know-how, so ask around if you'd like some support.
- Pace yourself. Change happens fast when it comes to computing, but do you really need to be at the forefront? Aim to know enough for your needs. After all, if you don't use it, you'll lose it.
- Spend time getting to know the key websites that serve education in your country and others. Sign up for emailed newsletters and update notifications.

EXAMPLE INFORMATION EXPLOSION

I am totally blown away by the amount of information there is available for teachers on the Internet. I started teaching a decade ago, and it was nothing like that then. Used effectively, this can dramatically cut workload. I just wish it'd been there when I was desperately struggling through my first few years!

(Primary teacher with ten years' experience)

Under-utilisation of skills

This may not seem like it's an obvious stressor, but consider this scenario. You're employed in a school to teach the year group you specialise best in, but instead of being asked to co-ordinate your major subject you have to co-ordinate one that you have little specialist knowledge of. Stress levels rocket as your workload is unnecessarily increased owing to this inappropriate deployment.

Quick pointers

If this, or something similar, is your experience, these ideas may help:

- Speak to your senior management team about your concerns.
- Aim to determine whether there would be a possibility of swapping responsibilities with someone more suited to the role(s) you've been asked to perform.
- Make it clear that you are not wanting to reduce your responsibilities; rather, you'd like to pursue those that are most suited to your knowledge, skills and experience.
- Be honest about what you can offer your school. Push the things that you can achieve with most ease and that will not see you burning the midnight oil with piles of additional preparation.

The deepest principle of human nature is the craving to be accepted.
(William James)

EXAMPLE PURE FRUSTRATION

What is the point in asking an exercise-phobic to take a tennis class in the summer term? Watching Wimbledon does not mean you know how to teach the game. I'm a qualified tennis coach as well as being a maths teacher, and what do I end up teaching? ICT! Apparently it's 'pretty close' to maths. It's so frustrating. Schools can be their own worst enemies.

(Secondary teacher with eight years' experience)

CHAPTER 4

Well-being and stress in teaching – the hidden causes

To a great extent, this is purely subjective, but when teachers are consulted about the sources of the negative stress that they experience, common so-called 'hidden' themes recur.

Although this is by no means an exhaustive list, these are some of the less obvious causes of negative stress in the teaching profession.

The teaching psyche

Several reflective texts on the nature of teaching refer to the fact that teachers have to reach so far inside themselves to find solutions to the many challenges they are presented with each day that it can become impossible to separate problems in the classroom or with some other aspect of the job from problems or issues of a more personal nature. In other words, the point at which the professional persona meets the private persona blurs, and boundaries become indistinct, leading to an inability to separate the demands of the job from the wider demands of life in general. The inevitable outcome is burnout.

The solution to this is not to ensure that all teachers create clear distinctions between their teaching persona and their home-life persona, which would certainly lead to the creation of automatons in the classroom. Rather, there is a need to help teachers to handle the flow of emotional attachment to, and involvement in, the job, while holding back enough of their 'inner being' to keep a hold on the whole person.

EXAMPLE LOOKING FORWARD

I once read in a book that teaching is an inward-looking career in that teachers have to draw so much from their inner being when in the classroom that what happens between us and pupils can seem incredibly important – almost overly so. It's so hard to switch off when you are using sheer force of personality to teach and discipline pupils. What's going on in my life can't fail to have an impact on my teaching, and what happens to me in my classroom has a direct effect on my other life. Sometimes they seem so enmeshed it's impossible to see the wood for the trees. It's so easy to lose yourself in a job like this.

(Secondary teacher with two years' experience)

Quick pointers

- Every time you say, 'I am a teacher', remember that this is just a fraction of your personal 'story'.
- Good teaching cannot be described through a series of bullet points seeking to define 'technique'. It emerges through the blend of an individual's personal integrity and identity. The key is to recognise this blend while still being able to determine its constituent parts.
- What happens to you during the course of your professional life will inevitably have an impact on your personal life but does not need to crush, dominate or even have a permanently adverse effect on your personal identity.

The emotional attachment of teaching

Small wonder, then, that teaching tugs at the heart, opens the heart, even breaks the heart – and the more one loves teaching, the more heartbreaking it can be. The courage to teach is the courage to keep one's heart open in those very moments when the heart is asked to hold more than it is able so that teacher and students and subject can be woven into the fabric of community that learning, and living, require.

(Parker J Palmer, *The Courage to Teach*, page 11)

It's a brave man or woman who speaks of the inner life of a teacher, but to ignore this dimension of our life, especially when considering a notion such as well-being, would be folly.

A negative stress that seems to hit the profession with such force is the emotional attachment that teachers can develop to the craft of teaching and the minds and lives that are influenced so much. Retaining enough of one-self to remain attached yet not overwhelmed is essential.

Quick pointers

- Significant job satisfaction comes from feeling, even knowing, that what you do in the classroom *matters.* The balance is to be had when we can accept that we can retain emotional integrity, or wholeness, without falling headlong into an emotionally draining attachment to the job.
- Acknowledging that we have personal limits as well as possibilities can provide us with a degree of protection from the somewhat vulnerable position that a job such as teaching can, at times, put us in.
- The ability to reflect is the greatest skill a teacher can have, especially one who is in danger of suffering negative effects of an emotional attachment to the job. External factors are rarely the cause here.

EXAMPLE THE TEAR FACTOR

If anyone tries to suggest that teaching isn't an emotional activity, I won't believe them. When a child actually 'gets' what you're trying to teach them, when pennies drop and you can see learning take place, that will often bring me to tears. It's then that I know that I'm in the right job. And then a lesson is destroyed by a couple of kids who are so, so angry, and you know for a fact that nothing you can ever teach them will change their world view; that, too, brings me to tears. Then I really doubt if I'm doing the right thing because, well, what practical difference can I make?

(Primary teacher with five years' experience)

The public image of teachers

There's a gap between social reality and certainly some of the public's perception of teachers and teaching as a profession. Fuelled by a lack of understanding of what the job entails and the pay and conditions, cries of 'But it's only a short day' and 'Think of the holidays' can still prevail.

From this fundamentally cynical viewpoint, any attempts by the profession to improve conditions and promote the well-being of teachers may be seen as whingeing or carping. It's not helpful, but no one could deny that it occurs. Sadly, one of the most destructive effects of this particular public image is a crushing depletion in the self-esteem of teachers.

The public image of teachers is not by any means overwhelmingly bad. Most people who are directly involved in education, either as a school employee or as a parent or child have extremely positive perspectives on the job and those who do it. But the public image of the profession is something that requires near-constant attention to ensure that the job is reflected accurately in the media and elsewhere.

EXAMPLE FEELING DEFENSIVE

I find it incredibly infuriating to read negative comments about teachers in the press or to see teachers being blamed for all of society's ills in the media. We are not responsible for bad parenting. We cannot correct overnight the effect of using the TV as a babysitter. I sound angry about this because I am. And whenever teachers try to defend themselves they are branded as incorrigible moaners. The fact remains, many wouldn't even attempt to do what we do and we deserve to be supported, not targeted.

(Primary teacher with five years' experience)

Quick pointers

If you ever feel that your self-esteem is affected by an apparent public lack of acknowledgement of the job that you do, consider these points:

- Your *self*-esteem should not be influenced by another individual or organisation. Positive self-esteem has to come from within and not be dependent upon anyone or anything else.

- That said, it can be effective to do what you can to boost the self-esteem of colleagues when appropriate. If this becomes the habit in your school, you'll soon be reminding each other of why you should all have high self-esteem. We can never bank on positive feedback from others, but the more it happens in a school, the more likely it is to happen to you.
- Give yourself a news holiday. Don't listen to the television or the radio, or read the educational press, if you know it will serve to wind you up. For every negative or misleading headline you read, think of your own to counteract it. This is not to deny that there aren't sometimes improvements to be made; it is to provide a sense of balance and realism. Rarely is anything wholly bad.

ACTION Have you ever found yourself saying 'I'm just a teacher'? Why? What's *your* perception of the job? Write down at least ten reasons to be utterly proud of what you do. Be sure to read this list often!

Fear of being 'found out'

So much of what teachers do in the classroom in front of pupils is 'performance'. There's a growing trend towards 'edutainment' such that subject knowledge and the ability to convey this can, on occasion, take a back seat in favour of the slick and swish packaging a lesson can be delivered in.

While this packaging can be an incredibly effective tool in winning over unmotivated classes or gaining points in the popularity stakes, it is not, at the end of the day, what *matters* in the classroom. It will not replace solid teaching methods and cannot be used in place of building strong and durable relationships with those we teach. It will not cover gaps in knowledge or self-perceived ineptitude.

Quick pointers

- 'Performance' of schools in general, and of individual teachers in their own classrooms specifically, is a powerful motivator and driving force behind what schools do and achieve, but it is a double-edged sword if teachers seek to 'perform' to compensate for perceived weaknesses.

When this happens, fear is the driver, not a desire to improve from a successful base.

- Remember that pupils can learn from an incredibly wide range of learning experiences. That means that every lesson you offer them, no matter how swish or 'boring' you perceive it to be, will be packed with opportunities for development to take place.
- When preparing a particularly complex or innovative way of delivering knowledge, ask yourself: What is my motivation here? Be absolutely honest with yourself over whether fear, in any shape or form, might be a contributing factor.

EXAMPLE BEING FOUND OUT

It took me two years and a near nervous breakdown to realise that I was terrified of being 'found out'. I felt constantly worried about my level of subject knowledge and thought that if I spent hours each day devising zippy-wow lessons no one would ever know. You've probably never seen anyone so slick in the classroom, but that hid so much insecurity. For all the time I spent, I wouldn't say my kids had significantly better opportunities to learn than any others, but I got myself in such a state about it. I felt that I couldn't let go and had to keep on and on pulling out amazing lessons. That's such rubbish. A bit like thinking a friend will only like you if you keep taking them out to dinner. Well, I've learned that the hard way and am much happier for it and so glad I did it so early in my career. The truth is, all teachers have an insecurity over something. I now know that I'm not the only one who isn't perfect, and my teaching has never been better!

(Secondary teacher with three years' experience)

Limited opportunities for reflection

The pace of the teaching profession is such that there is little or no time to 'stand and stare'. Yet failure to do this is undoubtedly one of the major reasons why personal well-being deteriorates in any job, let alone in teaching.

Quick pointers

- It is essential to know *how* to talk to yourself. Finding solitude, writing a diary, walking alone, exercising, praying, meditating and even talking to a trusted friend or loved one are all ways of interacting with oneself.
- Talking to oneself is one thing, learning to listen to the responses is another! What are your gut instincts and reactions telling you? How urgently do you need to respond to them?
- Problem-solving is not the only goal when using reflective practices. Sometimes the aim will simply be to establish if everything is OK.

EXAMPLE   A DAILY DIARY

I now write a diary. If anyone had suggested to me just six months ago that I would ever say that, I'd have laughed! How the hell does a teacher have the time to sit down and handwrite a diary?! But it's the best thing I've ever done. I'd be horrified if anyone ever read it, but the very act of writing those thoughts and feelings down seems to generate a response within me. It's as if I'm now my own client and counsellor. It hasn't taken time from my life to do this. It's given me back time. I don't find myself doing the washing-up and having an angry conversation with my headteacher in my mind. I'm not telling pupils off in my sleep any more. It has become the signal of the end of the working day for me, and the discipline of it is now really natural, like brushing my teeth or taking a shower. I've tried to encourage other teachers to do the same but don't think I've been successful. But, for me, I can't rave enough about what it has done for me. I even turn to it at the weekends sometimes. At the very least it has shown me that inside me I do actually have a concerned and resourceful 'inner me'.

(Primary teacher with fifteen years' experience)

ACTION   What do you value in life? This is a crucial question to ask yourself, especially when you are in a job that demands so much physically, mentally and emotionally, and that leaves so little time for reflection. Think about your personal views towards honesty, integrity, giving and receiving, and so on. Does your job support these core beliefs of yours?

Reluctance to seek help

It is a trait of many skilled and competent professionals not to seek help when perhaps they most need it. Teachers are not the only group to show signs of this reluctance; it seems to be prevalent within the healthcare sector, too. Perhaps a contributing factor to this situation is the level of competence that the job demands. Teachers are so used to being the ones who handle whatever is thrown at them on an hour-by-hour basis. When it comes to maintaining personal and professional well-being, the advice and support of a variety of agencies and professionals will really serve you well.

Quick pointers

- Act promptly when you consider that your well-being is under threat. Appropriate advice sooner rather than later will prevent a downward spiral of confidence.
- Never be lulled into thinking that, as a professional, you must tackle everything your job demands of you alone. This is simply not the case.

ABOUT TAKING TIME OFF

Recent research from Sweden found that people who struggle in to work when feeling either physically or mentally unwell don't recuperate properly. This leads to them needing to take more time off in the long run and a greater amount of time feeling unwell. Not surprisingly, the study found that teachers, nurses, childminders and carers had the highest rates of turning up for work when sick. Yet these were also the groups with the poorest long-term health, presenting with mild depression, back pain and fatigue with high frequency. If you need a day off to support your physical or mental health, take it. You'll end up being absent for less time in the long run.

- Be aware of the possible sources of help that are there for you. These will include your union, Teacher Support Line, your professional mentor (if you have one), counsellors provided by your local education authority, books, the Internet (including support services provided by websites such as www.eteach.com and www.bullyonline.org), your doctor or other healthcare provider, and your family and friends.

EXAMPLE   NEEDING SUPPORT

An old friend of mine from teacher training days went through a terrible time when her school got a new head. When she told me the kinds of things she'd been through I told her to seek support for workplace bullying. I'd heard that these things can happen in schools – in every workplace, I suppose – but I didn't ever anticipate that she'd have so much of her confidence knocked out of her. She didn't even think she had a right to seek help and certainly didn't think there was anyone out there who would fight for her. Bullying is so destructive. Before I watched what happened to her I had no idea how easy it is to lose all perspective, and it was almost as if she just crumbled into herself. I had to tell her almost every day that she doesn't have to fight alone and that others will support her. Teachers should never feel alone. Perhaps we're all just too good at not asking for help.

(Primary teacher with fifteen years' experience)

Isolation

To be a teacher is not perhaps an obviously lonely job; but, for some, teaching in schools where a sense of togetherness and camaraderie is not actively encouraged and supported can be an isolating experience. This is thought to be due to the amount of time teachers spend performing their job with little if any communication with other adults. Bonds and relationships may be developed with children, but the influence of colleagues is apparently far more transient in some schools.

While it's impossible to change the ethos of a school when it comes to the social isolation of its teachers, there are some steps that you can take if you experience loneliness at work.

Quick pointers

- Seek out other staff whenever you get a moment. Even if this is just for a quick chat, it's valuable social interaction.

- Talk about your experiences with friends and family. OK, they won't want teacher talk all the time, but it's important that you express the way you are feeling.
- Visit Internet virtual staffrooms such as the one at www.eteach.com. This will put you in instant touch with other teachers from different schools and is a valuable way of gaining perspective.
- Approach your headteacher about ways in which the staff at your school might become more socially cohesive. This needn't involve going out on staff jollies; just a little more social interaction at the start and end of the day can be a step in the right direction.

EXAMPLE FEELING LONELY

How on earth could I feel lonely? I was never on my own! There were always kids and hustle and bustle, but I had very few friends on the staff. No one ever sat and chatted. No one asked me how things were going unless it was my mentor, and she made it clear that was her *job*. I never imagined that teaching would be a lonely job, but that's my experience so far.

(Secondary NQT)

The need for perfection

We all have a need for perfection to a greater or lesser extent, depending on what it means for us. For some, it will involve needing to be the best teacher they can be, the most organised and efficient, the one gaining the best results, and so on. For others, this need for perfection may bleed into other areas of life such as being the best daughter, son, wife, husband, mother or father, or seeking perfection in the home, or in finances or any other aspect of life.

Perfectionists often place incredibly unrealistic demands on themselves and on others. They expect thorough competence at all times and are unforgiving of bad days, often punishing themselves for 'getting it so wrong'. They want events to turn out exactly the way they plan and are usually ill-prepared for deviation in this.

EXAMPLE   PERFECTIONISM

I know I'm a perfectionist – always have been. Problem is, teaching is just about the worst profession to be in if you are a perfectionist because you never ever get to the end of the list of things to do. And your plans for the perfect lesson cannot take into account the full range of responses from the children you teach. You might plan the perfect lesson, be in the perfect mood to teach it, be perfectly prepared in every way, but for some reason the kids don't want to know. How do you respond to that? I usually blame myself for not predicting their behaviour. You end up beating yourself up about it and vowing to try harder next time. Where's the use in that? I envy those teachers who can just shrug their shoulders and say: 'Oh well, let's hope it goes down better next time.'

(Primary teacher with ten years' experience)

Quick pointers

- Check yourself every time you project your own need for perfection on to others. Not everyone works like that, and the perfectionists and non-perfectionists could probably learn a thing or two from each other!
- The next time you're planning, or producing resources for the classroom, give yourself a time limit. Experiment with this idea, and if you find yourself craving more time, write down how you will improve the resources or planning when you come to review them.
- Think carefully about how you're interpreting what's expected of you. Could there be a different interpretation?

Anxiety is the dizziness of freedom.

(Soren Kierkegaard)

Happy the man who has broken the chains which hurt the mind, and has given up worrying once and for all.

(Ovid)

ACTION Are you a perfectionist? Do you find it hard to let a task go? Do you give yourself a hard time when you know you could have achieved something better? Do you get frustrated at having to move on to the next task before the current one is completed to your satisfaction?

If you answered positively to any of these questions, you just might be working with perfectionist traits. While facing these and actively reducing their impact on your life is best done with professional help, you can do one thing for yourself. The next time you force yourself into giving 100 per cent at the expense of your overall well-being, stop yourself. Give 80 per cent and see what happens. It is possible to give yourself a break like this with no ill-effects.

Aggressive parents, colleagues or pupils

Fortunately, it's still relatively rare for teachers to come across physical aggression in the workplace, but certainly anecdotal evidence seems to be pointing to the fact that this is a growing problem. Whether the aggression is a challenge to authority – for example, parents defending their little angels – or simply the venting of anger because you happen to be in the firing line, aggression is never acceptable and should not be tolerated by schools.

It can be terrifying to face someone who so obviously is expressing anger directly at you, especially if this person is a parent, not least because teaching as a concept can only be truly effective with the support of those who influence a child the most, in other words, their parents or primary carers. When this support for teachers and for education in general is removed by parents, the battle for teachers is most certainly an uphill one.

Quick pointers

If you find yourself dealing with anger and aggression in the workplace, whether this is manifested physically or emotionally, these ideas may help:

- Move the discussion into a public area. Do not continue the conversation if you are not visible to colleagues.
- Suggest that a third party be present for the discussion so that you have a witness to events.

- Ask that you arrange another time to meet when the conversation can be more constructive. If this happens, make sure that you are not alone.
- Never be tempted to retract what you need to say for fear of making matters worse. Simply reiterate the issue and what you see as being a working solution.
- Aim for the conversation to take place when you are both seated as this will help to prevent it from escalating into physical violence.
- Aim to build on a sense of partnership in dealing with the issue in hand. This will clearly not be possible if the other person is angry but it is certainly a goal to work towards in the future. There is no harm in explaining exactly why you need their co-operation.
- Your school needs to be safe, and to protect its students and staff, but it also needs to be accessible to parents. Don't be tempted to avoid contact with parents, but make sure that you put your personal safety first.
- If you think that an interaction with a parent has been violent or abusive, report the matter through the appropriate channels in your school immediately. Write down the precise details of what happened, including any witnesses there may be, as soon as possible afterwards.
- If you are a victim of physical or verbal abuse, it is perfectly reasonable to expect unwavering support from your school managers, local authority and, if relevant, the police.

Each of us needs to withdraw from the cares which will not withdraw from us.

(Maya Angelou)

We are being judged by a new yardstick: not just by how smart we are, but also by how well we handle ourselves and each other.

(David Goleman)

We need human qualities such as moral scruples, compassion and humanity. These are accessible only through forceful individual development.

(His Holiness the Dalai Lama)

EXAMPLE SOUNDING OFF

I'd been given a message during the day that one boy's father wanted to talk to me about a detention I'd given his son. I knew he'd be trouble because of his reputation but I hadn't had time to arrange for someone else to be there because as soon as I dismissed the class he barged in. He started off by shouting, so I knew I should just let it wash over me until he stopped. Every time he drew breath I invited him to sit down as I thought that would calm him. Eventually he did, and I was able to talk. I kept it really quiet and told him that I understood that his son's detention was not the only cause of his anger. I guess that was a risky strategy, but it was clearly the last straw rather than the only problem in his life. I suggested that we move into the head's office as I knew he'd be there, and from that point my head took over. Interestingly, the boy witnessed his dad shouting at me; and I was dreading him being smug about it, but he wasn't. He actually apologised the next day and, believe it or not, our relationship is better because of the incident. If there's one thing I'd say to other teachers in this position, it's to get a witness in the room for your own safety as soon as you can, even if that means walking away from them while they're shouting at you.

(Primary teacher with eight years' experience)

An ideal

The characteristics of an 'ideal' working environment for teachers have previously been identified as:

- shared goals and high expectations to create strong communal identity
- respectful and dignified treatment as professionals by superiors and by parents and students
- participation by teachers in the decisions affecting their work
- regular opportunities for interaction and sharing with colleagues that promote a collective identity
- recognition and rewards for effort and achievement
- opportunities for professional growth
- decent working conditions.

ACTION Would you add anything to the listed characteristics of an ideal working environment?

Does your own working environment fall short in any way? If so, how?

CHAPTER 5

All about communication

Communication: the successful conveying or sharing of ideas and feelings.

(The New Oxford Dictionary of English)

Too often, teachers can feel isolated in what they do; too busy to seek perspectives and too wary to reveal their fears. Without an established and well-used habit in staffrooms of encouraging discussion about what's going on in teachers' lives, this isolation can become crippling, and the lack of dynamic interaction with others a paralysing force.

Fortunately, there are spaces outside school walls in which teachers can communicate – to air their views, request help and advice, or simply to rant. These spaces are mostly to be found on the Internet on websites such as www.eteach.com and www.teachernet.gov.uk. While these opportunities for teachers to interact in this way are crucially important – the extent to which they are used is testament to the immense need for them – it is still essential for teachers, and indeed all members of a school's community, to communicate as effectively as possible on a day-to-day, one-to-one basis.

ABOUT THE CONSEQUENCES OF FAILED COMMUNICATION

If we don't think and rethink about the way in which we achieve successful communication, there will be costs to bear. We will undoubtedly lose:

- time
- confidence
- respect
- trust
- possibilities
- opportunities
- collaboration
- motivation
- understanding
- shared information

These costs are too high in a workplace seeking to reduce the burden of work resting on the shoulders of teachers.

Communication with colleagues

If you are seeking to improve your experience of well-being at work, the way in which you communicate with your colleagues will play a crucial role. Be aware of the many ways in which you communicate with others, through speech and through non-verbal cues.

No one, Eleanor Roosevelt said, can make you feel inferior without your consent. Never give it.

(Marian Wright Edelman)

The greatest difficulty with communication is the illusion that it has taken place.

(R Marrotta)

EXAMPLE SPEAKING PARTNERS

We have 'speaking partners' at school. Every teacher is teamed up with another, and we talk about the job and how we are feeling about it on our terms. There is no agenda here, no performance management, no competition or anything draining like that. It is purely for us. We even invite our speaking partners in to observe lessons if we have a particular problem with a class. We agree a focus for observation beforehand and then talk about it after. It works really well and is very empowering for staff. We're sorting out our own problems without being inspected or appraised, and so on, and we're not afraid of having someone else in our classrooms. There's no pressure on us from above to do this – we do it because we want to. It doesn't feel like something to fear, and it certainly isn't risky, because we trust our speaking partners; it's a gesture of mutual support. Plus, it's brought the whole staff together; we're a much more cohesive unit since we brought in speaking partners.

(Secondary teacher with four years' experience)

You can't depend on your judgement when your imagination is out of focus.

(Mark Twain)

If you wait until you feel assertive before you tackle a particular situation, you'll probably never do it.

(Anne Dickson)

I will always have fears, but I need not be my fears – for there are other places in my inner landscape from which I can speak and act.

(Parker J Palmer)

If you want to be respected, the great thing is to respect yourself.

(Fyodor Dostoyevsky)

ABOUT HOW YOU PROCESS INFORMATION

In his book *Communicate to Win* (see Further Reading), Richard Denny explains that a person's predominant sense will have an impact on the way in which they process information. Apparently, we will use either visual, kinaesthetic or auditory cue-phrases depending on which sense predominates. Denny explains the following:

- Visual cue-phrases: 'see the sense'; 'looks to me like', 'appears to me'; 'short-sighted', 'see eye to eye'. Predominantly visual people normally speak fairly quickly, because they think in pictures. They try to make the speed of their words keep up with the speed of the pictures in their mind. They may greet you by saying 'Nice to see you'.
- Kinaesthetic cue-phrases: 'it feels right', 'get to grips with', 'hand in hand'; 'slipped my mind', 'let's lay the cards on the table'. Predominantly kinaesthetic types normally speak fairly slowly, because they are reacting to their feelings and sometimes have trouble finding the right words to match those feelings. They may greet you by saying 'How are you?', which of course means 'How are you feeling?'.
- Auditory cue-phrases: 'I hear what you're saying', 'loud and clear'; 'unheard of', 'word for word'. Predominantly auditory people also speak fairly slowly with a well-modulated voice, using words carefully and selectively. They may greet you with 'I heard you were coming today', or they may say 'I hear the job's going well'.

When two people share the same predominant sense they can generally communicate more easily. So when you become aware that the person with whom you need to communicate obviously has a different predominant sense from you, change the language you use in order to reach more effective communication. The more you listen to the words they use, the easier the switch will become.

Portraying yourself in the best light

There will be times when you need others to listen to you and act on your words. Perhaps you need help with a task, or have to negotiate with a colleague or manager about something. Whatever the scenario, the way in which you portray yourself generally will influence how positively (or negatively) your communications are received. These points are worth keeping in mind:

- Notice your colleagues. Take a moment to ask them about something close, or important, to them.
- Be friendly. Avoid sarcasm unless you know the other person so well you can be sure you will not be taken the wrong way. On balance, sarcasm is usually best avoided.
- Make others feel important; as though you are genuinely pleased to see and interact with them. Using a person's name will help to convey this.
- Take time to listen with care.
- Make a point of learning about those you work with most closely. Do they have children? What are their hobbies? What are their 'stories'?
- Be observant of those around you. Find the common ground between you and others.
- Show a little humility.
- Give credit where it's due.

Written communication

Often thought of as time-saving, the memo is relatively popular as a form of communication in schools. Whether this is scribbled on a scrap of paper and shoved into a pigeonhole or tray, or typed out on purposely designed stationery or via email, this potentially curt form of communication is here to stay. Pitfalls to avoid when writing memos include:

- Make sure what you write cannot be misconstrued. Read it and read it again. You know what you mean, but will others?
- Be brief but not curt.
- Use positive, not negative language.
- Make sure you'd be happy for what you write to be published.
- Don't only write to nag; a word of praise, thanks or congratulations is always welcome.

To free us from the expectations of others, to give us back to ourselves – there lies the great, singular power of self-respect.

(Joan Didion)

EXAMPLE MORE HASTE . . .

I had some money stolen from my classroom and I received a note in my tray from the head asking for 'the money and a list of the names of the children who may have been involved'. I wondered if he wanted me to repay the cash from my own purse, but he actually meant that he wanted to know precisely how much had been stolen. For a while he had me really stressed.

(Secondary NQT)

Assertiveness

Many people confuse being assertive with being aggressive. They often see someone who stands up for their rights, someone who demands fairness and equality, as being aggressive. Being assertive means affirming or being positive in your approach. Aggressive means to attack and to be on the offensive, often in an unprovoked incident.

From *Stress-free teaching* by Russell Joseph

As a method of communicating needs and opinions, assertiveness can be misunderstood. First described as a personality trait by an American psychologist as recently as 1949, assertiveness is not something that you either have or don't have, but it is something that can be encouraged and learned.

In her book *Developing Assertiveness* (see Further Reading), Anni Townend describes assertiveness as being primarily about self-confidence. In being honest with yourself and with others, you are respecting yourself and others. Being self-confident still leaves you open to the views of others even when they may differ from your own, and the ability to express yourself clearly means your views have the greatest chance of being heard.

Assertiveness, passiveness or aggressiveness?

There are clear and obvious distinctions between assertiveness, passiveness and aggressiveness, yet at times we all draw from each style, depending upon the situation in which we find ourselves. The key is to adopt an assertive stance more frequently than we do a passive or aggressive stance.

Passiveness

The person behaving passively does so out of the belief that they have no right to do otherwise. Their personal needs come so low in their priority ranking that just about everyone else they interact with, colleagues and pupils alike, are perceived as being of greater importance. Too bad if they disagree with the tasks they are asked to carry out; the passive person will simply get on with it without voicing their concerns or offering their suggestions as to how things could be done more effectively, or situations improved.

ACTION Are you ever:

- afraid to speak up in front of other people and wary of group situations?
- afraid of using direct language, or fearful of talking in anything other than a quiet, low-tone voice?
- reluctant to express an opinion, even a closely held one?
- resentful over the way situations turn out?
- reluctant to reveal true feelings, resorting to protective body language or simply being expressionless?

Have you ever recognised passive behaviour in a colleague? How did this make you respond? Were you more assertive? Did it make you feel aggressive? Were you able to support this colleague?

Keep your responses in mind as you read through the rest of this chapter.

Aggressiveness

Regardless of the motivations behind aggressive behaviour, it inevitably seeks to claim a 'victim'. In other words, aggressive behaviour involves communicating at the *expense* of another person.

An aggressive person may use the following tactics when communicating with others:

- employing a firm or loud tone of voice when talking on a one-to-one basis
- shouting down others
- using language to hurt or belittle others
- using intimidating body language such as invading personal space, aggressive facial expressions or staring with pointed eye-contact

---

ACTION You'll know if you've ever resorted to using aggressive traits when communicating with others. What can be more interesting to explore is whether or not you have witnessed an aggressive interaction between others. What happened? Did you feel anything about the aggressor and the victim? How might this interaction have better been executed?

Assertiveness

Assertiveness does not violate the rights of others. As a tool of communication, it is a form of self-expression that allows all parties to retain integrity and exhibit respect, while successfully conveying any truths that need expressing. It is about honest and appropriate communication.

According to the Fieldwork Online Training professional development course, 'Becoming More Assertive', people communicating assertively will often:

- initiate and end conversations when appropriate; they can also change the direction of a conversation if it is compromising their rights, feelings or opinions, while respecting the other person
- face up to and discuss issues and problems that are adversely affecting them
- question authority when appropriate
- openly express emotions and opinions
- say 'no' when too much is being asked of them
- use ordinary conversational tone in communication with others
- use respectful language to make a point
- match facial expression with the words spoken to avoid mixed messages
- use body language to indicate openness and friendliness
- engage and participate in group situations

ACTION How do you rate yourself against the list of characteristics of assertive people above? Does anything hit home as being a particular difficulty for you? Are you able to think of examples of when you have acted assertively and examples of when you would have liked to communicate more assertively? Keep these in mind as you read through the remainder of this chapter.

ABOUT BLOCKS TO ASSERTIVENESS

Considering the immense benefits to come from a community in which all feel entitled and equipped to communicate with each other in an assertive manner, it's a wonder that passiveness and aggression ever become features of the way in which we communicate. However, there are significant and powerful blocks to behaving assertively that can affect all of us at some stage.

The above-mentioned Fieldwork Online Training course identifies the following common beliefs that block assertiveness:

- that it's not OK to put yourself first
- that others' views must be accommodated before your own
- that asserting yourself will lead to others disliking you, or you offending others or appearing to be selfish
- that you must be sensitive to others and not vice versa
- that 'ought to' and 'should' take precedence over 'want to'
- that your position on any issue needs to be justified
- that you don't deserve recognition for your achievements
- that you are not necessarily the best judge of your feelings
- that it's not OK to ask for support and help
- that your mistakes will not be tolerated
- that it's not OK to change your mind
- that you can never be too empathetic

ACTION Having read through the list of common blocks to assertiveness, can you agree that any of these is adversely affecting your life and
well-being today? Make a list of the times in which you are most likely to
shy away from asserting yourself. What action can you take today to
change this? Read on for more ideas.

Developing your skills of assertion

Knowing *how* to communicate assertively is one thing. Actually carrying it
off is another matter, especially when you may be doubting your ability,
and right, to do so.

Keep these techniques in mind the next time you need to adopt assertive
communication skills:

- What you say and the way that you say it need to correspond so that
  you don't give mixed messages. Your body language and the words you
  choose should not betray in you a fear of being assertive. Use direct
  language and address the issues surrounding the *situation* and not
  the *individual*.
- Avoid being personal.
- Don't feel the need to over-apologise. If you have to explain why you
  cannot take on an additional task, you do not always need to apologise.
- Be specific about what your needs are. The more specific you are, the
  more likely it is that your needs will be met or that a workable
  compromise can be reached.
- Don't feel the need to offer extensive explanations about what you can
  and cannot achieve.
- Use 'I' statements when discussing your needs and opinions. 'It would
  be nice if there was more time to complete year 8 reports' is a vague
  statement. 'I would like some more time to complete my year 8 reports'
  is a different matter. You could then go on to explain when you expect
  the reports will not be completed.
- Repeat yourself over a period of time if it appears that no action has
  been taken in your favour, or no compromise worked towards. If you
  have to become a 'broken record', so be it.

EXAMPLE HOLDING YOUR NERVE

It is so ironic that I can assert myself in front of a class of twenty-five six-year-olds but when it comes to talking to my headteacher I crumble. How did I get this far in my life and still buckle at the thought of saying what I need, what would work best for me? Believe it or not, I have in the past agreed to things that I know wouldn't work just because I didn't have the guts to say as much. In the long run it's a complete waste of time. But I just think that every time I try to be assertive I come over as bossy. Perhaps that's how I've been made to feel. It's hard to hold your nerve when you're the baby in the staffroom.

(Primary NQT)

ABOUT ASSERTIVENESS AND WELL-BEING

In the school environment where communication with others is such a vital dimension of retaining control over the multifarious features of the job, anything that jeopardises your ability to assert yourself also threatens your personal and professional well-being. Being assertive is not an optional extra in a job that can seem open-ended and uncontained. If you are to achieve and maintain an overall sense of well-being when it comes to your work, you need to feel comfortable about when and how to assert your needs.

Saying 'No'

It's a common perception of those both inside and outside the profession that teachers simply must be assertive otherwise they wouldn't be able to do the job. This isn't automatically the case. Having the skill to guide a class through the knowledge and skills they need to acquire does not necessarily mean that teachers can assert their needs in every situation. Too many other factors come into play, not least the socialisation processes we go through in our formative years. Ask a group of teachers whether they ever feel 'put upon' and you are likely to receive a positive response from at least some of those asked.

There are four main reasons why teachers can find it hard to say 'No'. These are often emotional hooks that are held on to and are therefore hard to shake off:

- managers lead them to believe that they are obliged to complete the extra tasks in question
- they are insecure in their performance (regardless of whether this insecurity is well placed or not) and think that performing additional tasks as requested will improve their feelings of self-worth
- they want to create the impression that they are ready for anything
- they simply don't know *how* to say 'No'

These reasons are more destructive than positive.

If you feel that you need to say 'No' in response to a request from a colleague (or, indeed, anyone), it is far better to go ahead and say it than to accept the task or challenge and not have the time to deliver. This can add immeasurable negative stress to your life and frustrate the person who made the request of you.

When saying 'No':

- offer an explanation, but don't feel obliged to go into lengthy detail
- be aware of sending a consistent message; you're entitled to say 'No', but if you mutter it with a wince you'll undoubtedly get your arm twisted until you comply!
- say it with the belief that you are entitled to refuse the request and to have your needs considered; your tone does not need to be overly apologetic
- if possible (and appropriate), offer a practical suggestion that could be a compromise. For example, 'No, I'm sorry I won't be able to paint the set for the play, but I can pick up the paint on my way home from school if that would help.'
- remember, it is often the case that it is perfectly reasonable for additional requests to be made of you but it is also perfectly reasonable for you to decline to deliver when it is inconvenient for you. School communities thrive on a diet of give and take, but this has to flow all ways. Give, give, give solely on your part will ultimately do no one any favours, least of all you.

ACTION If the thought of saying 'No' to certain people or requests sends chills down your spine, spend a moment or two to script mentally what you would say the next time you are asked. If it would help, practise saying it in front of a mirror. Adopt an open stance (don't cross your legs or arms). Keep an eye on your facial expression to make sure you don't deliver your message with a frown or a sneer!

EXAMPLE AN IMPORTANT REALISATION

I actually think that one of the reasons I found – no, *find* – it hard to say 'No' is that on some level I believe that my relationships with certain colleagues are dependent upon me behaving in a certain way. I have never said 'No' to some of the staff in my school and I honestly think they wouldn't hear it if I did. What can I do with that?

(Primary teacher with three years' experience)

Making requests

Being assertive doesn't simply entail saying 'No' when the need arises. There will be many times that you need to make requests of others, and if you ever feel that these are rarely met this section may be of value to you.

- Don't be afraid to state exactly what your ideal outcome would be. If it isn't possible to achieve this, you at least have a starting-point from which negotiations can take off. For example, if the time you would spend with your class during an assembly would give you the opportunity to finish that last report in time for the deadline, you might want to ask the teacher who doesn't have a tutor group to help you out. If he will be occupied for part of the assembly, perhaps he can help you out for the remaining time. Compromises can be reached, but state your ideal first.
- Keep your language simple. State what you need, and if you use 'I' statements ('I'd really appreciate your help' and so on) you are personalising the situation. This can often appeal to the aspect of humans that likes to feel needed!

• Again, keep your body language open and friendly. If you're defensive in any way, you may appear to be closed to negotiation.

ACTION Take a moment to consider your attitude towards making requests of other people. Do you feel you have the right to:

• ask others to help you?
• express yourself?
• admit that a job would be better done by someone else or in collaboration with another?

If you can't answer positively to each of these questions, think about why this might be. What are your underlying core beliefs? How might these be affecting your well-being? What action can you take to change them?

Body language

> Mortals can keep no secret. If their lips are silent, they gossip with their fingertips; betrayal forces its way through every pore.
>
> Sigmund Freud

Body language can shout louder than any other form of communication, so utilise it and make it work for you. Some pretty staggering facts about our non-verbal interactions include:

• 70 per cent of all communication is visual rather than auditory
• we use some 750,000 signals
• we use 15,000 signals from the face alone

Being an effective communicator will ultimately promote and preserve your well-being in the workplace and elsewhere, so ensuring that you are giving yourself the best chance when it comes to interacting with others and understanding the way in which others communicate is essential.

Richard Denny, author of *Communicate to Win* (see Further Reading), explains that people should learn to listen consciously with their eyes. This means reading the signs that are presented, irrespective of the words that are said. For example, notice the gestures, postures, position and distances that people adopt.

Clothes, accessories and general appearance such as a new haircut or hair colour can have a dramatic impact on the way in which we present ourselves to the world. Just look at what happens as a result of a 'makeover'! Support yourself in your communication with others by considering how you come over to others. Do you present to the world the person you want to be?

Body language pointers

- Calm eye-contact is essential when interacting with others unless the conversation is particularly casual; it's one of the most effective ways of conveying that you are offering your full attention. In doing this, you can expect full attention in return.
- Watch for signs of boredom in those you interact with. Don't be alarmed at this; we all reveal boredom at times, or let slip through our body language that we don't have time to listen any longer, or that we really should be doing something else. Just be aware that your message may not be heard if the person you are speaking to is rest-less or edgy. On the other hand, if they lean towards you, pull their chair in closer or smile and nod in agreement regularly, that might be the time to wade in with that request you've been meaning to make.
- Extroverts tend to be tactile people, but touching another, particularly in a workplace interaction, may not be well received.
- Defensive signals include folding your arms, slouching, crossing your legs, fidgeting and holding something such as a book or a folder across your body.
- Smiling will help you feel at ease and will show your willingness to listen to others. Apparently, all primates 'smile' in greeting!

EXAMPLE ACCEPTING BAD HABITS

It wasn't until I saw myself on video during a twilight training course that I realised how much I touch my hair when I'm talking to others. It even annoyed me when I watched the tape. I really hope I can train myself not to do that – it's not the image I want to have.

(Primary NQT)

Coping with conflict

Conflict is unavoidable and doesn't always need to be regrettable. It's through conflict that solutions are sought often in an accelerated manner; without the crisis of the conflict, the need for resolution is less urgent.

That said, conflict can still create unpleasant atmospheres in the workplace, affecting some more profoundly than others. We cannot eliminate conflict, but there are ways in which it can be dealt with to ensure the best all-round results.

When dealing with a conflict situation keep these thoughts in mind:

- Aim for a win–win solution. This is not a time for point-scoring.
- State the situation as it appears from your perspective. Explain that this is your perspective; you are not claiming the view as an indisputable truth.
- Give your reasons for wanting to reach consensus.
- Offer possible solutions. Compromise from each 'side' is most likely to result in a win–win outcome.

ACTION Take a moment to think about a situation you have been involved in recently, either at work or outside, where a conflict of opinion was an issue. Was a solution or consensus ever reached? How did you feel about it? If you were not able to reach consensus, have you been left with a feeling that there is unfinished business? How important is it to you that conflicts are resolved? Can you see how conflict affects your sense of well-being?

The Teacher Support Network has identified seven distinct types of difficult behaviour and the strategies that can be employed when faced with them. These types of behaviour are as follows.

Know-it-alls

Symptoms

Apparently very confident, the condescension implicit in this behaviour is hard not to resent. A know-it-all may actually know what they are talking about, but they can equally fake or falsify knowledge to maintain the same aura of invincibility. The know-it-all, however, usually tolerates no opposition, admits no other opinion.

Coping

'Be prepared' is the key motto here. Make sure that you have a solid grasp of all key facts. State your position in a less dogmatic, more open way but be careful with correcting errors; leave them a way of saving face.

This coping strategy is, at first sight, submissive, but the key aim is to get the over-confident person to accept you so that you can work together. Controlling a situation does not always involve being dominant.

Moaners

Symptoms

Complainers have some easily noticeable traits in common. They often are people who are very comfortable in the way they themselves do things but who feel powerless to change the issue at hand. They will often be very prescriptive, so that any deviation from their accepted norm is automatically a source of complaint. Complainers rarely offer solutions, however, as a solution may involve challenging their own perfection.

Coping

The best initial strategy is often to take the moaner at his or her own self-worth. Listen carefully to the complaint and summarise it back to show that you have understood it. You can then throw the complaint back at the person by asking for solutions: 'What do you want to happen?' 'How would you handle this?'

You therefore engage the moaner in the conflict-resolution process and force the person to look for positive responses.

> Sometimes I go about in pity for myself, and all the while a great wind is bearing me across the sky.
>
> (Ojibwa saying)

Procrastinators

Symptoms

Delay and indecision characterise the procrastinator, but this does not necessarily imply weakness. Apparently indecisive people can often have a particular solution in mind, and they use stalling tactics until they get their way, or they may simply be unable to represent their actual position confidently. There is often a high level of sensitivity to external opinion with such people.

Coping

Procrastinators will often need your active support to bring out the reasons for their indecision. You have to work to make communication easy for the person and instil confidence that they will be listened to. Try to avoid putting such a person on the spot; having drawn them out, actively work with the person towards a solution.

Bullies

Symptoms

Hostility, anger, selfishness are all qualities associated with the bully. They can work out in the open, where what you see is what you get, or they can be insidious, hiding behind social norms but still being aggressive, confident and attempting to assert dominance. Sometimes this can take physical expression.

Coping

Bullies try to overwhelm opposition, so you have to state your point cogently and with confidence but non-aggressively. Give them the opportunity to say their piece: let the bully run out of steam, bring the person hiding on the side into centre stage. If the person is in danger of getting physical, keep eye-contact and try to get the person seated. You will need to take the person seriously, and almost always you will have to deal with the issue raised there and then. To that extent, the bully may be perceived as having got his or her way, but the key issue for you is to discuss rationally the point in a way with which you feel comfortable.

Persistent or serious bullying is a form of harassment and covered by legislation. If you have tried reasonable measures to cope with the bully and have had little or no success, you can take more formal action, either by yourself or with the help of colleagues. Keeping a record of your attempts to deal with the bully may be helpful later. If your school has an anti-harassment policy, you should read it before deciding the best action to take. With any such case, you can get guidance and support from Teacher Support Line and your professional association. Being on the receiving end of bullying behaviour is never pleasant and can be very stressful. You do not need to be alone as you consider your best options and develop your coping skills.

The quiet ones

Symptoms

These people handle difficult situations by shutting down, withdrawing all but the basic minimum communication methods. This can be aggressive as well as defensive behaviour, deliberately withholding a response to sabotage the process. The key difficulty is that, because of the withdrawal of communication, you have less evidence on which to base your assessment of the reasons for the behaviour.

Coping

You need to provoke some sort of response, so you should ask open questions, ones which cannot be answered simply by 'Yes' or 'No'. You may need to invest a good deal of time in this process. When they finally do open up, engage with the person actively but sympathetically; let them steer for a while.

If no response is forthcoming, end the situation yourself and arrange another time for a meeting. Do let the person know what actions you intend to take as a result of the meeting.

Killjoys

Symptoms

You will often have difficulty with someone who disagrees with anything you put forward, and sometimes even with the process itself. Often, such a person actively seeks to pick holes in whatever is presented, just for the sake of it. This person may have some personal issues, but in work-related cases such an attitude is often linked to a feeling of powerlessness and disappointment.

Coping

The main strategy is to accept their pessimism while promoting optimism yourself. You can also raise potential problems and negative points yourself, so as to pre-empt negative comment. Make sure all points are discussed before promoting your own solution. But ultimately you may need to be prepared to take action on your own.

Nice people

Symptoms

Nice people cause difficulties, too. Someone can be personally agreeable, apparently sincere and supportive, but will they deliver? For them, keeping everyone happy can be more important than dealing with solutions.

Coping

Since these people have a need to be liked, show that you like them. Then you can actually begin to address the issues. Often this means dealing with personal matters before the real issue at hand, such as enquiring after family. Often nice people make a lot of jokes, which can hide deeper issues, so listen carefully to them.

Nothing on earth consumes a man more quickly than the passion of resentment.

(Friedrich Wilhelm Nietzsche)

People seldom want to walk over you until you lie down.

(Elmer Wheeler)

EXAMPLE CONFLICT RESOLUTION

There was one guy in my school that I just clashed with. It wasn't anything unpleasant, but I just knew that every time he opened his mouth I'd get annoyed by whatever he said. It got to the point where I'd automatically discount his opinion, and that was quite damaging for our professional relationship; we have to present a united front to the kids at least. We had so many public disagreements over the smallest of things, and I started imagining that all sorts of hidden messages were embedded in what he said to and about me. I was actually scared of confronting him as I felt that he'd have the support of others if anyone got to know about it because he's been at the school longer than me, but at the end of the day I had to do something. We've actually got to the point where we can enjoy sparring off each other. We're much more supportive of each other even though we cannot always agree, but that tension has been dissipated, thank goodness.

(Secondary teacher with three years' experience)

Most of the time, the trait against which we are reacting in another is something within ourselves that we do not accept.

(Alan Cohen)

If you are patient in one moment of anger, you will escape a hundred days of sorrow.

(Chinese proverb)

When we can no longer change a situation, we are challenged to change ourselves.

(Victor Frankl)

The person who knows how to laugh at himself will never cease to be amused.

(Shirley Maclaine)

ABOUT 'DIFFICULT' MANAGERS

All teachers have to juggle complex relationships every day; it's part of the job, and an ability to do that is probably part of the reason why you became a teacher in the first place.

But problems undoubtedly arise when the school managers you have to work with exhibit behaviour that's difficult to respond to. For example:

- If your headteacher or other members of the school's management team are perceived as ineffective or weak, this can become a source of conflict.
- If your headteacher or other managers are perceived as dictatorial, steam-rolling over the needs of others, you may feel disempowered, especially if the goalposts are continually shifting and you don't know where you stand.
- If you perceive that support is not forthcoming when it should be, you can be left feeling vulnerable and frustrated.
- If you think that your headteacher may be working to a hidden agenda, such as wanting to redeploy you in the school performing a different role, or wanting you to leave altogether, feelings of negative stress are bound to take over.

Of course not all teachers are in conflict with their managers, but being able to recognise when you are is a significant part of reaching a solution. Whether your experience of your managers is something only you feel, or whether it is a common experience of many teachers at your school, action does need to be taken. The common responses to conflict involve the following:

Collaboration: everyone is involved in reaching a solution that meets all needs: the ideal situation.
Compromise: everyone is involved in reaching a solution that meets some but not all needs.
Decisive: a decision is taken which ignores some members of the group.
Avoidance: nothing gets done.

Whatever approach you take in raising the issues that concern you, aim for collaboration if at all possible.

Feedback

A significant part of our communications with others in the school setting involves giving and receiving feedback. Whether you are communicating with adults (colleagues or parents) or pupils, these ideas may help:

Giving feedback

- Be sure that you are clear in your intentions for the feedback. It should be objective, not subjective.
- Honesty has to be the best policy, but raw truths can be packaged to ensure that the message is received (and to protect fragile egos!). Offer specific examples to back up what you are saying.
- Respect the need for confidentiality.
- Offer eye-contact and be aware of how your tone of voice and body language could be interpreted by the listener.
- Avoid any language that could be construed as humiliating.
- Make a clear distinction between facts and opinions.
- Allow time for the receiver to speak and offer their opinion. Repeat your message in response if it becomes clear that you have not been heard.
- Move towards finding solutions and identifying sources of help and advice as soon as possible in the conversation.

Receiving feedback

- Accept compliments with grace. There's no need for modesty when you've achieved good things!
- Aim to determine what the person giving you the feedback intends. What is the purpose behind it?
- Be aware of the power of language. Have you over- or under-reacted to anything?
- If you disagree vehemently with anything you are told, take a moment or two to compose your thoughts before saying anything. A well thought out response will serve you better than resisting the natural temptation to fire back with personal justifications. Never leave unreasonable criticisms to fester unchallenged.

EXAMPLE IN TOO DEEP

I was acting head of department for a term, and one of the deputies was effectively under me in the department. I found myself in the really awkward situation of having to observe his teaching as part of some departmental evaluations we were doing. Fortunately, he didn't act like my boss in that situation and even offered suggestions of things he felt I should feed back to him about. It's a strange part of the job that sometimes throws up mixed feelings in me. My assertiveness was tested then, and I learned quite a lot about how dialogue between adults in the school situation should be. I'm very grateful to him for that.

(Secondary teacher with two years' experience)

Golden rules of communication with colleagues

Most of the time your communications with others will flow with ease; but there may be times when hiccups occur, and the way in which you respond to these will have an impact on the overall outcome. These points may prove useful:

- If you have a valid reason to 'moan', there will be appropriate routes through which to make this known so a solution can be sought. This might be through discussing the gripe with your line manager or mentor, or adding it anonymously to a suggestions box. Whatever you do, don't bash on about it incessantly in the staffroom! It may sound obvious, but even when others agree with our moans, they won't necessarily want to hear about them.
- Observe how you feel about certain styles of communication. Watch how others interact and notice if you behave differently when in the company of particular colleagues. This all helps to determine how best to communicate with others for the best possible outcome.
- Be true to yourself in your interactions. Coming from a point of stability and honesty is important, even when you don't perceive all others doing so.

- Keep an eye on the style of language you use in your communications with others. Subtle changes in the words we use can have an impact on the way in which our message is received. For example, do you ever exaggerate to make a point? Do you focus on the problems and not on the potential solutions? Is there a willingness for flexibility in your language? Do you use limiting words?
- Show others that you are able to see the pros and the cons of a situation.
- Don't let conflict situations slide without making the effort to resolve them sooner rather than later.

ACTION Whenever you find yourself reacting to someone or to a situation in an emotional way, stop and ask yourself these questions:

- Imagine watching yourself as you speak. Are you embarrassed by what you see and by what you hear? Are you impressed? Does it entertain you or sadden you?
- Do you think the situation will matter in a year's time? In two years' time? In five years' time? If not, consider your response very carefully. Is this something you can walk away from, dignity intact?
- Would you want this discussion recorded and replayed? Would you want it discussed after your death?
- Can you explain your stance to all of those you love? Would they understand your perspective?

CHAPTER 6

Enhancing personal well-being at school

A key thought, albeit an over-simplification, that should sit at the root of any attempts to improve your sense of well-being at school is that work, at its most basic level, is about your role in the world. There is always a bigger perspective that we shouldn't lose sight of. When we do, feelings of futility can emerge.

One thing that seems consistent across all the literature concerning coping with negative stress is that there is little consensus on what this actually means! For the purposes of this book, *coping* has been taken to mean enhancing that which reduces the impact of negative stress. The natural pay-off should be an improvement in personal well-being (and, by default, in that of the school, too).

Yet, rather than coping, the goal should surely be thriving. In minimising stress and maximising the chances of well-being, it is hoped that the best outcome can be achieved: an outcome that sees you enthusiastic about your work, balanced in mind and healthy in body.

One comes to be of just such stuff as that on which the mind is set.
(Upanishads)

Out of clutter, find simplicity
From discord, find harmony
In the middle of difficulty lies opportunity

(Albert Einstein)

ABOUT YOUR 'COPING STYLE'

The way in which you respond to potential stressors will have a direct impact on the overall effect the stressor has on your body and life.

In his book *Flow*, Mihaly Csikszentmihalyi identifies three kinds of resource available to us in the face of negative stress. These are:

- the external support available
- your psychological resources such as intelligence, education and personality factors
- the coping strategies that you use

The third point in this list is the most important in our control of the other two points.

Csikszentmihalyi goes on to explain that there are two main ways that people respond to stress:

- the positive response is referred to as a 'mature defence'
- the negative response has been called a 'neutotic defence' or 'regressive coping'

It's impossible for one person to respond fully positively or negatively. Most of us fall somewhere between the two, depending on our resistance at the time the stressor strikes. But it's worth remembering the words of Csikszentmihalyi: 'The ability to take misfortune and make something good come of it is a very rare gift. Those who possess it are called "survivors" and are said to have "resilience", or "courage".'

There is certainly such a thing as a resilient personality. These people are typified by their energy, enthusiasm and idealism. They don't continually *react* to the circumstances they find themselves in; rather, they are able to take the events of their life and transform them to progress their lives further. Resilient types are very much of the belief that 'what doesn't kill you makes you stronger'! They don't want to *cope* or simply muddle through. They need to thrive, to remain optimistic and powerful in their job and fully connected to why it is that they do what they do.

ACTION Think about when you last demonstrated 'resilience'. When did you bounce back from adversity, drawing the positive from a seemingly negative situation? Is this something that comes easily to you? Why, or why not?

EXAMPLE RESILIENCE

People have described me as resilient but I'm not sure that's quite right. I just can't bear the fact that sometimes things happen that are seemingly out of your control. I have to make sense of life as I go through it, and the thought of being a 'victim' is abhorrent. So does that make me resilient? I just don't want to waste life's experiences, good or bad.

(Primary teacher with two years' experience)

Although not always possible, it is useful if you can take a fairly systematic and rational approach to your pursuit of well-being. Above all else, symptoms should be dealt with sooner rather than later. One thing that is certain is that effective early help can prevent all kinds of negative long-term effects, and may even constitute the difference between you staying in a profession that you love and leaving prematurely because it cannot sustain your well-being. And, if you think you seem to be the only one affected by negative stress and the impact it can have on your well-being, just know that you are not alone. Take a look around your staff-room. Are you honestly the only stressed person?

ACTION The survivor traits of resiliency, flexibility and adaptability are crucial not only to happiness within the teaching profession, but to happiness in life, too. Jot down the aspects of your character that show these traits, and take a moment or two to appreciate the scope of your being. And remember – there is nothing wrong with paradoxes!

> **ABOUT** ENHANCING PERSONAL WELL-BEING AT SCHOOL
>
> As far as possible, consider these factors when seeking to enhance your well-being at school:
>
> - negative stress should be eliminated or minimised at source where possible to prevent problems from escalating
> - positive action should be taken as soon as symptoms of negative stress arise
> - keep a close eye on well-being issues; this is not something that can be solved with a magic bullet – your personal well-being needs constant nurturing.

Emotional literacy

Teaching is an inherently emotional profession. In fact, emotion is at its heart. Yet not all teachers, and indeed other professionals, are happy to agree with this. As Dorothy Rowe wrote in her book *Guide to Life* (see Further Reading), 'Emotion is meaning. Unfortunately, many philosophers, psychologists and therapists haven't realised this.'

We don't have a definitive theory of emotion, and if you ask more than one person to define the term you'll get more than one answer. But this need not necessarily confuse the issue. The important factor is the extent to which you can utilise your own emotional literacy to enhance your overall sense of well-being.

> **ACTION** What do you understand by the term 'emotion'?
>
> How does it differ from 'moods' and 'feelings'?
>
> What are your typical emotions? What do you find yourself experiencing most often?

EXAMPLE QUESTIONS, EVEN FOR GOOD SCHOOLS

I went to a whole day's training on well-being, and we were asked these questions. Apparently they were devised so that any school could ask them, even if they considered themselves 'a good school'. I think they work equally well when you ask them of individual teachers. It helps them to think about the role that their own emotional literacy is playing in their day-to-day lives and whether they could enhance their well-being by paying more attention to them. These were the questions; I ask myself them all the time:

How active is listening in the school?
Who feels heard and unheard at the school?
What opportunities are there for discussion and debate?
Is emotional literacy given a high priority in planning?
What are the predominant teaching and learning styles?
What is actively done to empower the formation of good relationships?
(Secondary teacher with five years' experience)

Many thinkers on the notion of emotional literacy point to the fact that teachers can only achieve great things with the emotional literacy of their pupils to the extent that they understand and utilise their own emotional understanding. There are several tests available for assessing your emotional literacy, and a quick search on the Internet will provide you with plenty of ideas, but the thoughts below may help, too.

In his book *Working with Emotional Intelligence* (see Further Reading), Daniel Goleman refers to the idea that self-awareness is a vital foundation skill for the following:

Emotional awareness: recognising one's emotions and their effects
Accurate self-assessment: knowing one's inner resources, abilities and limits
Self-confidence: a strong sense of one's self-worth and capabilities

Goleman explains that people with emotional awareness know which emotions they are feeling and why. They recognise the link between their feelings and their actions and conversations, and can see how their emotions affect their performance.

Those with the skills of accurate self-assessment, explains Goleman, are aware of their strengths and weaknesses. They learn from experience through reflection and are open to feedback, new suggestions and horizons, and the need for continuous lifelong learning. They are also able to show a sense of humour about themselves.

The self-confident, Goleman believes, are able to present themselves with self-assurance and have 'presence'. They are able to voice views that may be unpopular and can go out on a limb for what is right. Those with self-confidence are decisive and can make sound decisions despite what else may be going on around them.

ACTION Going on these brief descriptions of some of the elements of emotional literacy, how would you assess yourself?

Do you have emotional awareness?
Can you perform accurate self-assessments of yourself?
Are you self-confident?
Be honest! Is there anything you would like to work on to improve your level of emotional literacy?

Goleman also refers to self-regulation (the ability to manage your internal states, impulses and resources), motivation (the emotional tendencies that guide or facilitate reaching goals), empathy (awareness of others' feelings, needs and concerns) and social skills (adeptness at inducing desirable responses in others).

When taking care of your emotional well-being at school, remember these points:

- We all experience fluctuations in our emotions throughout the day. No one is ever happy, sad, angry, disappointed and so on *all* the time. Whatever emotion you experience while at work, know that it will pass.
- Never react with a fiery retort to either colleagues or pupils without first considering whether you will be proud of yourself once the emotion has passed.

- Aim to identify your emotions. Give them a label and acknowledge them as they arise. Recognise if they take you away from your sense of balance in yourself.
- At the earliest opportunity give time to any emotions that are causing you difficulty. For example, if you are angry with a colleague or a pupil, you will need to communicate with them to reach a workable understanding.
- Do not allow problematic emotions to linger unchecked. Keep a sense of perspective. If a situation or event has upset you, don't transfer that to other people or situations.
- Seek help with your emotions if they overwhelm you. The easiest way to do this is to discuss how you are feeling with a trusted colleague or friend. If you would like to do this confidentially, talk to a counsellor.
- You are not your emotions. You may typically feel certain emotions as a result of particular events, but you do not have to become the embodiment of them. They do not have to rule your life.
- Be aware of when your emotional reserves are running low. If you are feeling uncharacteristically tearful, sarcastic, angry or irritable, you may need to recharge your batteries. Don't forget that it's not just for physical ill-health that you can take days off. Your mental health needs nurturing, too.
- While expressing yourself as literally as a child does is inappropriate in the adult world, what we can learn from the way children express themselves is honesty and integrity. Ultimately, emotional literacy allows for us to stay true to both of these.

Do what you can with what you have where you are.
(Theodore Roosevelt)

Work and recreation belong together like eye and lid.
(Rabindranath Tagore)

Look, it's silly for you to come home from work miserable every day. Why don't you just stay there?
(Woman greeting husband at the door in a 'New Yorker' cartoon)

ABOUT MANAGING EMOTIONS

In his book *Nurturing Emotional Literacy* (see Further Reading), Peter Sharp describes how the way that feelings are handled or managed is crucial to developing emotional literacy. If you are adept at managing emotions, it doesn't mean that what you experience is any less than what others experience. The person who rants their anger loud and clear is not necessarily feeling it more keenly than anyone else; rather, they are expressing it in a less constructive way.

Taking responsibility for your emotions is essential. Largely, we are not *made* to feel a certain way by others, but *allow* ourselves to feel that way for a variety of reasons. When day-to-day feelings and emotions overwhelm us, we have to take steps to handle them more effectively.

Managing emotions does not mean squashing them down until they're nestling deep within. It means appropriately expressing them, even using them, to bring about positive change in our circumstances. And don't, above all else, give yourself a hard time about appearing inconsistent or contradictory. As Walt Whitman observed, we contain multitudes!

To explore the ideas of emotional literacy in more depth, start with the work of Daniel Goleman and Peter Sharp (see Further Reading) or visit the website: www.antidote.org.uk

He who fights with monsters might take care lest he thereby become a monster. And if you gaze for long into an abyss, the abyss gazes also into you.

(Friedrich Wilhelm Nietzsche)

You will never find time for anything. You must make it.

(Charles Buxton)

One ought, every day at least, to hear a little song, read a good poem, see a fine picture, and, if it were possible, to speak a few reasonable words.

(JW von Goethe)

EXAMPLE BEING OVERWHELMED

I know that teachers are supposed to be in better control, but when this incident happened I was a trainee and emotionally and physically exhausted. Every waking minute of each day was taken up with school-work, and I had no reserves left. The actual incident that took place was just small – the straw that broke the camel's back really – but I found myself bursting into tears when my mentor asked me in the corridor how things were going. He whisked me into a nearby office and sat me down. He totally understood the exhaustion I was feeling and got me to the point where I could gather my thoughts and look at resolving the issue. He helped me do that before I went home. He insisted that I took the night off, and I felt so much better for the release of it all. I know what my warning signs are and I try to listen to them, but it's not always possible. In such an emotion-centred profession they are bound to get the better of some of us occasionally.

(Secondary teacher with five years' experience)

Workplace bullying

There is a clear difference between bullying and strong management. All managers have the responsibility and authority to address the behaviour or work performance of an employee, but this must be done in accordance with proper procedure. A sign of good management is how nurtured and encouraged you feel after a 'pep talk'. If you are left feeling despondent or humiliated, it is likely that bullying tactics have been employed.

All managers must observe the work of their employees and offer constructive advice on potential improvements should the need arise. This is, in fact, an obligation of management. The obligation of employees is to take on board what has been said and to strive to work towards improvements. There are, however, tell-tale signs of bully-tolerant institutions which all exhibit:

- high absenteeism
- high turnover of staff
- low morale
- a sub-culture of disrespect towards management

EXAMPLE   BULLYING HEAD

It is such a pleasure to sit in a staff meeting and actually be able to contribute to the proceedings! I could never have done that with the last head. We just had to sit still and shut up! But now my views were actually sought and listened to. She even made notes from what I said. It's such a relief not to be discounted like we all were before she started working here.

(Primary teacher with twelve years' experience)

Identifying what bullying is

It is important to establish a definition of bullying as opposed to a personality clash or a difference of opinion. True bullying can involve:

- insidious, relentless, destructive criticism
- trivial fault-finding
- humiliation and ridicule, both private and public, designed to put down rather than to nurture improvement
- excessive work expectations with unrealistic goals and deadlines
- abuse of discipline and competence procedures
- inappropriate forms of communication (e.g. shouting, ordering, ignoring or 'death by a thousand memos')
- inexcusable blocks to promotion or training
- withholding of recognition for performance, sidelining and marginalising; making an employee feel 'irrelevant' and ignored within an organisation
- manipulation, or singling out for 'special' treatment
- lack of compassion in difficult circumstances
- inappropriate bad language or offensive remarks
- obstructing an employee's work through denying them the full information necessary to do a job
- starving an employee of resources
- imbalance between responsibility and authority
- excessive and inappropriate monitoring
- encouragement to feel guilt

Dealing with bullies: an action plan

If you are experiencing bullying at work, there are many things that you can do to minimise its ill-effects. This action plan has been designed to help teachers to take the initial steps towards dealing with workplace bullying.

- Talk to a trusted friend or loved one about your experiences. A second opinion will really help you to retain a sense of perspective about the situation and will help you to decide whether to take further action.
- Reread your job description and any other National Standards that might apply to you. There will be other information available in your school on the responsibilities of teachers. This will reaffirm what tasks you should and should not be performing in your job.
- Attend an assertiveness course, or read about it. Chapter 5, 'All about communication', carries extensive advice on developing assertiveness. It is particularly important to hone these skills as your professionalism may be under question and you will need to be able to deal with it calmly and rationally. Confidential professional counselling would also be a good idea at this stage. This is available from Teacher Support Line (08000 562 561 in England and 08000 085 5088 for Teacher Support Cymru). Counselling may also be available from your LEA. Retaining a perspective on the situation is crucial to the way in which you approach your bully. Try to prevent the situation permeating every aspect of your life.
- Seek advice from your professional association. Bullying destroys good teaching, and you don't want to be facing accusations of incompetence in addition to the bullying. Most professional associations have their own documents on dealing with workplace bullying, which are available to members and non-members.
- Ask for a copy of your school's policy on workplace bullying.
- Read about workplace bullying. There are some excellent books available (see Further Reading), and these will serve to assure you that you are not alone; this problem is widespread in workplaces generally.
- Gather support for your cause by speaking to carefully selected colleagues. Divulge a little of what is happening to you and you may find that other members of staff come forward as sufferers, too.
- Document all communication you have had with your bully – even relatively informal contacts. This is not being unnecessarily paranoid

and will certainly serve you well should you need to refer to these records at a later stage. Taking this action is simply helping to avoid unnecessary stress and anxiety.

- Refute all unfair claims that have been made against you – in writing if necessary – and keep records of anything you say or write.
- Monitor changes in your work performance due to bullying. This might include getting behind on marking and preparation, or feeling inhibited in your teaching. Keep copies of any induction assessments, performance management appraisals and inspection reports you may have had and read all the positive comments when your confidence is low.
- Visit your healthcare provider even if your health doesn't appear to be suffering. It is sensible to have formally recorded what is happening to you and whom you consider to be responsible. Your healthcare provider will be able to offer constructive stress-busting advice and will be a source of support should you need to take time off school. If sick leave is recommended, follow this advice. Time taken sooner rather than later could prevent a health crisis. You should record any ill health resulting from bullying in your school's accident/incident book.
- Never be encouraged to 'slide out gracefully' or to leave the profession if that is not what you want to do.

Time management

A universal experience of teaching is a lack of time. All over the world, time-poor teachers are struggling to do more in every hour than some workers hope to achieve in a day.

You have to know what your working style is if you are to be able to manage your time more effectively. There are many books on the market that can help you to determine this, so browse around your local library or good-quality bookshop for some ideas. The Further Reading section on page 201 has some recommendations, too.

Time management is a learned skill, although some people take to it far more easily than others. That said, there are some time-management fundamentals that you can put to immediate use in attempting to tame your workload and get through your tasks:

- Be realistic. You can't do everything, so don't even try.
- Establish what your long-, medium- and short-term goals are. Be sure to devote time to these so that you can be successful in achieving them.
- Write your plans down. Make lists of jobs and, again, divide them into long-, medium- and short-term tasks.
- Guard against procrastination. If you sense you are avoiding a task, choose a different one that is smaller and readily achievable; but, as soon as that task is done, do at least something to make a start on the job you've been putting off. The minute you start it, it'll diminish in stature.
- Skim-read documents that do not require detailed analysis.
- Keep your workspace clean and clear. Get into good habits of processing paper efficiently, and of filtering the information that comes your way. Either file it for future reference, put it in your 'recycle bin' from where you can retrieve it if necessary (although be sure to empty this bin regularly), or throw it away.
- When you are given a task to do that will severely eat into your time, compromising your ability to complete other existing tasks, talk to your line manager. It may not be necessary to refuse to do the task, but you will need to negotiate either time or resources to assist you. Again, be realistic in what you set out to achieve. Realism is not a sign of failure.
- Delegate tasks if you are able to. There are no prizes for doing everything yourself when you simply don't need to. Besides, control freaks are not good team players.
- Minimise the risk of interruptions by not attempting to work somewhere public like the staffroom. Just a few breaks to chat, and your concentration is split and attention divided.
- When something seems unachievable, divide it into small chunks of manageable goals. Tackle just one thing at a time. Remember, divided attention leads to tension.
- Reduce or cut out unnecessary tasks.
- What are your most productive times in the day? Plan to get the bulk of your tasks done in those hours. Many teachers report experiencing a slump in energy once the pupils have left in the afternoon. If you experience a distinct lack of get up and go at around 4 o'clock, eat some dried fruit for quick energy release and have a drink of water along with whatever else you would normally drink at this time.

- Be sure to build some slack time into your long-term planning. It's perfectly natural to need time to catch up, but don't see your holidays as the time to do this.
- Make use of printed or computerised planners/diaries/schedulers.
- Spend time at the start of the school year creating time-saving systems such as templates for any letters you will need to send out, filing systems, record-keeping systems, and so on.
- Collaborate with others whenever you can. If you can minimise all your respective workloads by working together as much as possible, all involved will benefit.
- Be sensitive to overloading yourself. There's no heroism in this kind of martyrdom.
- Stick to schedules or negotiate extensions.
- Limit your availability by turning off your mobile phone and not downloading emails when you have a specific task to complete. The fewer distractions you have, the quicker the task is done and you can have some quality time off.
- Analyse your use of time. Do you typically leak time during your working day?
- Pay attention to the sense of balance in your life. It's no good being perfect at time management at work while struggling with it at home.
- Drop any pretences to perfection. There really isn't any such thing.
- Above all else, hone your skills of assertion and say 'No' whenever you know that your well-being will be adversely or irreparably affected. There should at least be the opportunity to discuss your concerns.

ACTION Think about your relationship with time. Do you have enough time to complete the tasks you want to complete or are you always running against the clock? Are you in control or does time control you?

ACTION Do a quick mental audit of the workload facing you right now. Focus and prioritise. What is essential and urgent? Do these things. Anything else, even if deemed important, can wait. You have to allow yourself to categorise and prioritise in this way.

EXAMPLE THE STEADY PLODDER

I don't really know how I have lasted so long in teaching because I am definitely what you'd describe as a 'steady plodder'. I'm more than happy to work day after day but I get through my work like the tortoise and not the hare. But teaching seems to demand incredibly fast bursts of energy regularly through the day. I have to resist this for my own sense of well-being. My sessions are pacey, but I don't burn myself out during each one.

(Primary teacher with ten years' experience)

These ideas will help you to develop time-management skills that work for you:

- Limit your availability. It is a fallacy that the more available you are to give out to your pupils and colleagues the better you are as a teacher.
- There's a temptation to put off the tasks you know you enjoy and tackle the grot first. If you go in for delayed gratification in this way, be sure to time-limit the jobs you really don't enjoy and be strict! Say to yourself: 'I will get this done in the next hour and no longer and will not be distracted.'
- Become a magpie. Ask people constantly about how they manage their time and pick and choose what techniques will suit you.
- If you find yourself with some unexpected spare time, don't fill it. Take a walk, curl up with a book or chat to colleagues, but don't feel you have to be 'productive'. Besides, using the time to chill out for a bit will probably be far more productive in the long run.

Whatever games are played with us, we must play no games with ourselves.

(Ralph Waldo Emerson)

Yesterday is history
Tomorrow is a mystery
Today is a gift . . .
That is why it is called the present.

(Author unknown)

EXAMPLE   GIVE YOURSELF A BREAK

I was watching a colleague in the staffroom the other day. She had a meal on a tray that she had brought in from the dining hall. She sat down, pushing the food to one side so that she could mark some books while she ate. Four times she got up to respond to queries from other people and pupils. Four times. Where are her boundaries? Why can't she even say 'I'm eating at the moment but I'll help you later'? Where is her sense of self-worth? It can't be in being so available that she can no longer eat a meal in peace! Is that what I'll be like when I've been in the profession for ten years? If it is, then I need to get out now, while I still see how crazy that is.

(Secondary teacher with two years' experience)

Pacing yourself

You have to be aware of the law of diminishing returns when managing your time. There will be an optimum level at which you can work effectively. Go beyond that level and you risk wasting your time and wearing yourself out. If your working hours are so long that you have to force yourself out of bed in the morning, ask yourself what it is that you hope to teach your pupils. If you feel depressed about your work, it is likely that you're not working at an optimal level and it is essential that you pace yourself to avoid burning out.

Every school year has a rhythm, just like every term, every week and every day. When you are in tune with this, you are more able to go up a gear when necessary, and to reduce the pace when it fits. It's impossible to work at 100 per cent all the time, racing through each term as it hits you; no one can achieve that successfully.

Aiming to work fewer hours when you are pacing yourself sensibly is not necessarily about doing less work or getting less done. Rather, it's about being more productive, if possible, in the time that you do spend working. The following ideas may help:

- When you decide to spend time on schoolwork, focus, and minimise all other distractions.
- Work out what it is that you like to do best and do that for the greater part of your time. You could even swap tasks with a colleague if it means you both spend time doing more of what you enjoy.

- Delegate as much as possible, or team up with colleagues to achieve tasks. There's no point in reinventing the wheel, or for two people to slave away at what could far quicker be achieved through teamwork.
- Time your tasks but be realistic with the deadlines that you impose on yourself. They should never become an additional source of stress.
- Do not feel that you have to work at the pace of those around you. Even if you are working closely together in one year group, department or faculty, you still have to work at your pace if your sense of well-being is to remain intact.
- Take a moment to consider if you have any time-wasting habits or inefficiencies. Try to develop a conscious awareness of how efficient you are when you are working.
- Take regular breaks from intense work such as marking.
- Practise 'mindfulness'. This means being aware of the present moment, of what you are doing and how you are doing it. This is quite the opposite of doing A while thinking of B and C. Practising mindfulness tends to have the effect of apparently expanding time.
- Be an *author* not an *actor*. This is your life, and its scenes should at least in part be directed by you. Don't play out someone else's lines at a pace that doesn't suit.

ACTION   If you think that you may not be working at your optimum pace, ask yourself these questions. If you answer 'Yes' to some or all of them you might want to explore time management in more detail:

- Do I avoid beginning tasks because it all seems like too much?
- Do I allow myself time to plan what needs to be done?
- Do I spend time on tasks that are not essential?
- Do I allow myself to be interrupted by colleagues and pupils?
- Do I help others to achieve tasks at the expense of my own work?
- Do I view deadlines as constructive encouragement or a source of unparalleled stress?
- Do I struggle with tasks that could or should be done by someone else?
- Do I underestimate how long something will take me?

ABOUT MINDFULNESS

Some religions espouse the benefits of mindfulness, or being mindful about the task in hand. The idea is that divided attention leads to tension. It is impossible to live in our society and be mindful all the time but one way of working towards this is consciously to focus on a job such as marking a class set of books. Set yourself a time limit and during that time don't answer the door or the phone; stick to the task in hand and minimise all other distractions. If your concentration wanders, have a thirty-second 'power' break and refocus until your time limit is up. This way, mindfulness becomes a learned discipline that you can apply to all aspects of your life. For example, when you are watching television, do just that; when you are washing your hair, focus solely on that process; and so on. The effects of negative stress cannot be felt through that level of concentration on a task.

Working with other adults in your classroom

There's no doubt that a sound working relationship with the other adults that may be involved in your classroom can do wonders for your sense of well-being at work. In order to utilise the assistance they can give you, consider these points:

- Make sure you know the reason the assistant is working with you. Read their job description and don't be tempted to push its boundaries without negotiating this between you first. Your roles should be clearly differentiated; but, as the Department for Education and Skills in England says, 'By definition, support for the teacher is at the heart of the role of the teaching assistant'.
- Go over in detail your classroom rules and routines. Your assistant will need to be fully involved in what happens in your room, and why.
- What, exactly, do you want them to do to help you out? (Staying within the scope of their job description.) Keep your overall well-being in mind when you think about this.
- Give your assistant sound feedback at regular intervals. It's teamwork that can make this relationship work, so devote time to it.

EXAMPLE

I have never had such a great working relationship with a classroom assistant as I have now. It has taken time to build up, but right from the start I decided that I was determined to see some positive benefit for myself. We meet regularly for no longer than fifteen minutes to go over work and plans, and I am confident enough to let go of some of the tasks like designing displays that I always used to do. We have talked about what she's good at and can do fairly easily and what I need help with. There's enough common ground there so it's win–win at the moment.

(Primary teacher with twenty years' experience)

Looking after your voice

It's little surprise that teachers as an occupational group are among the most likely to be referred to a speech therapist for help in minimising permanent voice damage. Of course susceptibility plays an important role, and you will not necessarily suffer, but being aware how you can protect your voice is invaluable. Common throat disorders that teachers seem to suffer from are pharyngitis, laryngitis, vocal-cord polyps, vocal-cord nodules and contact ulcers (sores on the mucus membrane covering the cartilages to which the vocal cords are attached).

If you've ever spent even part of a day with a rasping throat, unable to deliver the intensity in your voice that you'd wish, you'll know that teaching is far easier when you have fully functioning vocal cords! When you're in the classroom, your voice is the most valuable tool you have. Lose it and you rely, almost exclusively, on non-verbal communication. Unless your pupils are exceptionally compliant, understanding and forgiving, this simply won't be enough.

In order to produce sound you need to be relaxed. Believe it or not, the voice is part of the body's muscular system, which is why tension can often be heard in the voice. The more relaxed you are the stronger your voice will be.

Your posture can also have an adverse effect of your voice. The more hunched your shoulders are, the harder it is to breathe calmly and deeply. Without breath, there's no sound! Be aware, too, that your voice has its natural pitch, and straining above and below this when addressing a class will cause it damage. A good test to see where this is involves saying 'hmmm', and the sound you make is likely to be around your natural pitch.

Vocal threats

Threats to your voice abound throughout the school day, from the environmental factors found in your workspace such as a dry atmosphere, poor ventilation, board-pen fumes and chalkdust to background noise, needing to raise your voice above its natural level, and repeated and incessant use throughout the day. You really do owe it to yourself to take care of it.

Voice care

- Drink plenty of water all through the day. This will keep your throat lubricated.
- Warm your voice up before your teaching day begins.
- Develop non-verbal cues for your class(es) to follow. These could be standing in a particular place to issue instructions or clapping to get attention and so on. Before you open your mouth, think: Do I really need to do this?
- Avoid shouting in the classroom at all costs. It is terrible for your voice as well as being disturbing to others around you.
- Relax your neck and jaw as often as possible. Yawning is an excellent way of doing this. Aim to lower your shoulders as soon as they rise in tension.
- Don't drink spirits neat.
- Cut down on your intake of dairy produce to reduce the formation of mucus.
- Stop smoking! Avoid smoky atmospheres, too.
- Avoid clearing your throat. This action brings the vocal cords together very forcefully, risking damage.
- Get enough sleep.

You should consider seeking professional advice about your voice if you suffer repeated voice-loss or a substantial change in the quality of your voice that lasts for more than about two weeks.

Blood-sugar maintenance

'Blood sugar' refers to the level of glucose in the blood. Diabetes is characterised by high levels of blood sugar (hyperglycaemia), while hypoglycaemia relates to low levels of blood sugar.

Both hyperglycaemia and hypoglycaemia are relatively common in the Western world. They can each require medical intervention, so it is important to seek the advice of your chosen healthcare provider if you suspect you may be suffering. For the purposes of this book we will focus on low blood sugar.

There is a huge range of symptoms associated with low blood sugar, but the common ones cited by those who have experienced a crashing drop in blood sugar are:

- sweating
- shaking
- feeling irritable and confused
- feeling suddenly and ravenously hungry
- headaches
- cold extremities
- anxiety

These symptoms can be triggered by many factors, including:

- missing a meal
- excessive exercise that you are not accustomed to
- for women, the week or so leading up to a period
- excessive intake of sugar
- shock
- excessive alcohol intake

To avoid the symptoms of low blood sugar, when the brain is starved of glucose and your body is struggling to function with comfort, try these ideas:

- Eat little and often. Fortunately, the teaching day lends itself to snacking in this way, but it's important to snack on the right foods.
- Make sure that each snack consists of a combination of a carbohydrate and a first-class protein (for example, dairy produce, tofu, fish or white

meat). This combination of carbohydrate and protein produces the optimum rate of sugar release into the bloodstream, which sustains even energy levels over time.

- Avoid snacking on high-sugar snacks such as chocolate, biscuits, sweets, cakes and sugary drinks.

To find out more about low blood sugar, go to Further Reading.

Humour

There's a lot of truth in the phrase, 'Laugh and be well'. Now that we have a wealth of research and evidence on the positive benefits of laughter and humour, we know that to live a life without it would be flat, stifling and uninspiring, not to mention boringly tedious! Not only does humour make us feel more relaxed when we allow ourselves to laugh, but there are also actual physiological responses within our body that are as close to the reverse of our stress responses as it is possible to get. To borrow from a well-known comedian, our sixth sense is our sense of humour!

Why did laughter evolve?

If we look at laughter from a behaviourist viewpoint, it becomes clear that it is a social signal. Research has shown that we are thirty times more likely to laugh in social settings than when we are alone. We use laughter to strengthen social bonds, showing that we are comfortable with each other and willing to be free and open. Therefore, say researchers, the more laughter within a group of people, the closer the bonds are likely to be.

When this is related to the school setting, laughter between colleagues has to have a positive impact on the cohesiveness of the team. It is also likely to have a positive influence on the willingness staff members show for new and existing initiatives designed to raise school standards. After all, who wants to be left out of the feel-good factor?

There are few situations that cannot be eased by laughter. We see it, sub-consciously, as a disarming mechanism: a universally understood signal of trust. In fact, when we laugh, our fight-or-flight response is inhibited, making us vulnerable to attack, yet still we chortle because we feel safe enough to. We could, therefore, conclude that a school without laughter is a hostile environment.

There is a dark side to laughter, though. Just as a baby laughs when it is given what it wants, some believe laughter to be an act of aggression (however mild) where laughter equals winning and could well have originated from a cry of triumph on the defeat of a foe. We cannot get away from the fact that, however democratic a school may be in the way it is led and managed, there will be some dominant individuals who determine the tone and ethos of its environment. It's an old cliché, but one worth heeding, 'When the boss laughs, everyone laughs'!

The overriding proviso must be that any laughter within the school setting must be non-ridiculing *connecting* laughter if we are to glean the physiological, psychological and spiritual benefits we want from it.

How does laughter affect us?

Early studies of laughter and humour lent themselves to ridicule within the medical profession, yet still persistent believers strove to prove what they knew all along: that laughter has a beneficial, healthy effect on the body's immunity. The conclusion that laughter is a *eustress state* is now widely accepted.

After exposure to humour, this is what happens within the body:

- Natural killer cells increase in number and activity, strengthening immunity.
- The fight-or-flight *distress* response is suppressed in a reduction of stress hormones.
- The diaphragm receives an aerobic workout through laughter, increasing its ability to use oxygen.
- The effects of pain can be less pronounced as laughter offers a powerful distraction. One study saw patients being told one-liners after surgery and before painful medication was administered. Those exposed to humour perceived less pain than those who were not given the chance to laugh.
- The muscles involved in the act of laughing receive a workout; those not directly involved relax.
- Intellectual performance is boosted, particularly in the ability to retain information.

EXAMPLE FUN STUFF

We decided one year to start up a humour board when we were heading for an inspection. It was in the staffroom, and we all brought in funny cuttings, cartoons, pictures, and so on. It didn't take a minute to pin them up and there'd always be someone reading the board as they passed through. The inspection has long passed, but our humour board is still there. We won't get rid of it now; we're all too reliant on it!

(Secondary teacher with seven years' experience)

Many psychologists believe that humour helps individuals to confront personal problems in a more relaxed and creative state, generating heightened flexibility of thought.

If humour can enhance well-being as effectively as the research seems to indicate, we need more of it and we need it fast! Here are some ways of encouraging humour in schools:

- Share absurdities with one another.
- Use eye-contact and smiles as frequently as possible.
- Create a humorous thought for the day. This could be generated by any staff member and shared with pupils if appropriate.
- Emerson wrote that 'The earth laughs in flowers'. Can you use flowers in your school's environment? In the reception area perhaps, or the staffroom or classrooms.
- Keep cuttings of cartoons, misprints, funny stories and so on to put up in the staffroom. Be sure not to leave them up so long that staff members cease to notice them. Keep changing them so that staff members seek them out.
- Use cartoons around the school to help communicate important messages.
- Share embarrassing moments with each other.
- Laugh with others when they laugh.

ACTION Commit yourself to seeking out humour at least once each day. Even if this is just through chatting with colleagues, aim to laugh out loud whenever you can. Notice how it makes you feel and how it affects your thoughts. Laughter may not be a cure-all for everyone, but it just might do it for you.

Taking time off

There will be occasions when it is appropriate and necessary for you to take time off work. However, it can sometimes be easier for teachers to struggle through feelings of ill health rather than organise work so that they can take time to rest. Added to this is the burden of knowing that a colleague will probably lose valuable time in order to cover your class while you are at home.

Struggling on to avoid the guilt so often associated with taking time off can never be positive in the long run. Inconvenient as it may seem, taking a day sooner is infinitely preferable to needing a month off later.

Despite the fact that teachers are among those workers who have the highest rates of turning up to work when sick, if you do feel the need for time off, you're not alone by any means. In England, the proportion of state school teachers who took time off sick in 2002 stood at 57 per cent. Each teacher took an average of 5.3 days off.

If you need to have some time off, follow your school's procedures for this closely. Keep your headteacher informed and, if possible, anticipate how much time you will need off so that cover arrangements can be made. This isn't always possible, so don't worry if you can't be specific. When you're preparing to return to work after a long absence, always seek the advice of your professional association as you could inadvertently put your entitlement to holiday pay at stake.

Deep play helps us to feel balanced, creative, focused and at peace.
(Diane Ackerman)

ABOUT RETURNING TO WORK AFTER A STRESS-RELATED ABSENCE

Although the reason for your absence from school is essentially a matter between you and your chosen healthcare provider, if you are absent owing to a stress-related condition, it would be sensible to discuss this with your headteacher or principal. Your return needs to be carefully managed, and a reduced workload may be appropriate for the short term, even if that means you working part-time for a while.

If persistent sources of stress, such as unchallenged misbehaviour, remain after your return, then the likelihood of a regression in your sense of well-being is heightened.

You may want to consider temporarily scaling down your additional responsibilities at school if your post carries them, and should certainly consider passing on some of the other extras such as PTA membership, even if only for a while as you get back up and running.

Remember, the aim is not to return to how you used to function. The aim is to build up slowly until you can manage all aspects of your work in a manner that does not compromise your sense of personal well-being. You're heading for a sustainable approach to your work, not a return to burnout or similar.

If you want to be monitored on your progress, ask for a follow-up appointment with your headteacher to discuss how things are going. This can serve to reassure both parties and will also ensure you a time to discuss any ongoing concerns. Remember, the success of your return will depend to a great extent on the quality of your communication with managers and colleagues.

Counselling

There may be occasions when you feel that your well-being at school would be enhanced by being able to talk through the issues that concern you. Although counselling will be covered in more detail in Chapter 9, these steps may help if you are in this position:

- There is a difference between discussing concerns with family and friends and discussing them with a professional counsellor. Counselling offers a confidential space in which you explore problems and seek solutions. Many schools, professional associations and education authorities offer access to telephone counselling services, and these would be a good first port of call.

- Your healthcare provider may be able to refer you to a counsellor if they feel this would help you.
- Personal recommendation is always valuable when selecting counselling support. If you know anyone who has sought counselling, ask for an introduction or contact.

EXAMPLE TELEPHONE SUPPORT

I honestly don't know what I would have done that night if I hadn't picked up the phone and rung Teacher Support Line. I felt so low and uncharacteristically out of control. Trying to juggle so much at school, relationship difficulties at home and trying to look for a new house. I was overwhelmed but totally without energy. It was late at night, and I knew I couldn't face another day at school. Just half an hour on the phone was like breathing a massive sigh of relief. They didn't make it all better, but did show me how to take that first step to make things better for myself. It was that sense of empowerment, combined with practical advice and a sympathetic ear that gave me enough energy to face the next day. And, let's face it, that's all you need. Just that gentle hand to hold through the dark times that makes you believe you can do it. You can get through the coming days.

(Primary teacher with eight years' experience)

CHAPTER 7

Well-being and career development

If you're attempting to take a holistic view of your personal well-being, it's impossible to avoid focusing on your career development. That doesn't mean that you must strive ever onwards and upwards. Rather, it means providing yourself with the opportunities you need to be able to thrive in your job, at whatever level that may be.

Now is probably a good time to mention that all thoughts about your well-being as it relates to your career must be without 'oughts' and 'shoulds'. Don't compare yourself to others and feel that you should be as successful or as driven as they are. All that should concern you is how you *feel* about where you are in your career and what can be done, either by you or by others, to support your aspirations.

This is particularly important. As soon as you feel the weight of what you *should* be achieving or where you *ought* to have been promoted to by now you lose sight of where you actually *want* to be. Take heed of this advice from Henry David Thoreau:

> If a man does not keep pace with his companions perhaps it is because he hears a different drummer. Let him step to the music he hears, however measured or far away.

Listen to your drummer.

Keeping an eye on your career

Your success as an educator relies in no small way on the time and commitment you give to your continuing professional and personal development (it's impossible to distinguish between professional and personal development – the two are inextricably intertwined). In a profession such as teaching there is no option to stagnate, but it's surprising what emotions and limiting factors come into play when we think about our own professional development. It's easy to think we can't afford to take on further study, or it wouldn't be appreciated if we did, or we couldn't possibly spare the time or we'd really rather not progress any further.

The mental and intellectual well-being of teachers is closely linked to emotional well-being. It is usually emotional factors which limit our attitudes towards learning, and when these are combined with the limiting institutional attitudes towards personal and professional development that some schools struggle with it is no surprise that mental and intellectual well-being suffers.

Having a team of teachers who are committed to professional and personal development can greatly influence learning, increase staff morale and draw all elements of the school together in a common purpose.

Now, perhaps more than ever before, professional and personal development is part of the lifeblood of teachers. From the first day in the classroom and beyond, opportunities abound for those who want to define and refine where they are in the profession.

What we mean by professional development

> If a man empties his purse into his head
> No man can take it away from him
> An investment in knowledge
> Always pays the best interest.
> > Benjamin Franklin

Perhaps it's easier, first, to consider what professional development does *not* involve. It is not about competitiveness in the workplace, and it is not only reliant on quantifiable information. What it does require is co-operation between colleagues and the recognition of qualitative experience. In its broadest sense, continuing professional development refers to the enhancement of professional and pedagogic practice *throughout the duration of a teacher's career.*

ACTION Think about what your understanding is of continuing personal and professional development.

How broad is its scope?

How does your experience of development of this kind to date taint your approach to it for the future?

Do you know what your school's policy is on professional development? (Every school should have one.)

It's clear that professional development is gaining importance in today's world. From government departments to professional associations, from LEAs to individual schools, there is a sense that the aspirations of teachers need to be listened to and supported where possible.

ACTION Does the context in which you work actively support professional development?

Are you hindered in your attempts to develop yourself both personally and professionally?

Can you identify who or what hinders you?

Can you identify who or what supports you?

Opportunities for development

In her book *Continuing Professional Development* (see Further Reading), Anna Craft is keen to stress the wide range of methods of professional learning. These include:

- action research
- self-directed study as well as teacher research linked to awards such as masters and doctorates

- using distance-learning materials
- receiving and/or giving on-the-job coaching, mentoring or tutoring
- school-based and off-site courses of various lengths
- job shadowing and role rotation
- peer networks
- membership of a working party or task group (these may include what are sometimes called 'professional learning teams'; there are also 'learning partnerships', which may involve a range of different participants such as schools, LEAs and institutes of higher education)
- school cluster projects involving collaboration, development and sharing of experience and skills
- teacher placements including those in business but also in other schools
- personal reflection
- experimental 'assignments'
- collaborative learning
- learning mediated by information technology (for example, through email discussion groups, or self-study using multimedia resources)

ACTION From the list of possible opportunities for professional learning, which do you have most experience of?

Have you been able to determine which method of professional learning works best for you? Why is that?

Do you aim to be fully aware of when you are making professional connections and building relationships?

Do you know what opportunities for professional learning exist within your school? Within neighbouring schools? In conjunction with clusters of local schools?

Have you ever been able to implement in the classroom professional learning that you have acquired?

Twenty years from now you will be more disappointed by the things you didn't do than by the ones you did. So, throw off the bowlines, sail away from the safe harbour. Catch the trade winds in your sails. Explore. Dream. Discover.

(Mark Twain)

ABOUT THE IMPACT OF PROFESSIONAL DEVELOPMENT

It's hard to isolate the impact that the professional development under-taken by a teacher can have on a school's community. Primarily, it shows the teacher to be a model of lifelong learning, but it can also achieve the following:

- raise standards of achievement in pupils at all levels
- help teachers to manage change
- lead to the personal as well as the professional development of teachers
- improve the performance of individuals and institutions as a whole
- increase staff morale and sense of purpose
- promote a sense of job satisfaction
- pull together a school's vision for itself

It's important to ensure that you have a good idea about what develop-ment opportunities are open to you. It's not just a question of attending potentially dull and tedious twilight sessions when you're tired and your blood-sugar levels are about to plummet to an all-time low. Professional development is not a single event or moment in your career. It's a contin-uous process of professional and personal evolution.

The personal and professional development mindset

The mindset that encourages in you a drive to progress in your career (even if that means maintaining your current position) will undoubtedly enhance your mental and intellectual well-being. In fact, it could be said that a successful approach to professional development is dependent upon your attitude of mind. Regardless of any external factors that may impose limitations on you, the way in which you handle these will ensure you gain as much as you can from what's offered.

Factors which indicate the presence of a state of mind that is open to personal and professional development include:

- a willingness to seek out learning opportunities
- a willingness to see positive learning potential in all aspects of life
- an affinity with the process of reflecting on learning and change
- an overriding leaning towards curiosity about, rather than resistance to, change

There's such a wide range of situations that can offer teachers a chance to develop both personally and professionally, and being awake and alive to those will energise your work.

These points may offer some inspiration:

- Take a positive view of professional development. There's not a person on the planet who could not usefully be working towards furthering their professional expertise.
- Be flexible when it comes to dealing with the unexpected or with periods of uncertainty. This will enable you to glean maximum professional development from the situations with which you're presented.
- Regardless of how ambitious or otherwise your goals are, you deserve quality professional development – it's not just for other people!
- Once alert to the fact that professional development can happen every day, work at recognising just how much professional development your daily routine offers you.
- Be open about your desire for professional development. Make it known that you are lifelong learning personified!
- Be 'present' at meetings. Ask all the questions you need to ask there and then. Others will benefit from your questions and the answers they receive, too.
- Ask about any aspect of your work that is not crystal clear. This approach will engender an ongoing connection with learning and professional development that will be fundamental to all aspects of your work. Teachers are notorious for feeling that they should be able to cope with, and know how to deal with, every eventuality. This can lead to missed opportunities for development. You don't have to have all the answers all of the time.
- If you have a quest for perfection, drop it! There is no such thing as perfection, and attempting to pursue it may well stifle opportunities for development.

- Think about the ways you communicate with other members of staff. Are there opportunities for you to nurture the professional development of others through your communication? Are you approachable? (See Chapter 5 for more information on communication skills.)
- Be open about sharing information and resources.
- Collaborate whenever possible. Two heads can usually make lighter work of a task than one. Avoid being a lone ranger.
- Consciously observe the professional differences that exist between you and your colleagues. Do this from a position of interest, not from a position of judgement. How diverse is your staffroom?
- Never underestimate the benefits of networking – learning is infectious!
- How do you identify problems? Is it with possible solutions in mind, or simply for the sake of locating the problem?
- Be patient with yourself. Professional development is not about cramming all your goals into a short period of time. You need to set appropriate deadlines for yourself.
- Never compromise your work–life balance.
- Ask for feedback. Be specific about what you want and from whom.

Key factors in nurturing the mindset for development include:

- flexibility
- positivity
- ambition
- honesty
- receptivity
- unstifled realism
- communication
- collaboration
- patience
- balance

If we all did the things we're capable of doing, we would literally astound ourselves.

(*Thomas Edison*)

ACTION How effective is your school at encouraging a professional development mindset in its teachers?

Do you feel able to identify your needs at school? Do you recognise when your needs are met?

Are you fully aware of your motivations when it comes to professional development?

What do you do well? What advice can you pass on to others when appropriate?

The tension between personal and professional development

There's no doubt that all forms of personal and professional learning and development can have a positive impact on a school, but this does not negate the inevitable tension that will exist between individual and institutional priorities for development. These will be linked, but they are not interchangeable.

Put simply, the ambitions and targets of the individual would, in an ideal world, be perfectly matched to internally and externally perceived development needs. The institution will also have internally and externally perceived development needs that must reflect nationally imposed targets and obligations as well as reflecting the need for the school to be accountable for the education it provides.

In order to avoid damaging degrees of tension between the direction in which you, as an individual, want to travel and the direction in which others within your school would like you to develop, a balance needs to be sought. It's no good training to be a pastoral leader because it would really fit nicely with what your headteacher has in mind for you when what you truly have your heart set on is being a head of department. Responsibility for appropriate development must be accepted both by you as an individual and by the school or college in which you work.

ACTION Think about how your plans for future development might fit in with your school's development plan. Where might they differ? Can you determine any common ground?

EXAMPLE BEING PROACTIVE

I was so frustrated at not being able to pursue my goals when I wanted to. The courses that were offered to me weren't at all what I wanted to do, so eventually I took things into my own hands and found the kind of courses I was really interested in through adult education. It meant that I had to fund them myself; but I chose to do a counselling course, which has helped my classroom and behaviour management no end. My headteacher has noticed and did actually ask me all about the course. I think I'll carry on and get a counselling qualification, and I have been told that there may even be some funding for me if I do this. I have to make a presentation to the head about how this could benefit the school, but that won't be any problem!

(Secondary teacher with four years' experience)

Strategic career planning

If you're keeping a close eye on your career well-being, it would be wise to do some strategic career planning. Although this process may be helped or hindered by the situation in which you find yourself, there is still much to be had from thinking about where you are now and where you would like to be.

An important objective to bear in mind when planning your career is how can you apply what you have learned to your work? This, in turn, should be balanced by your personal development needs.

It's very difficult to draw up a plan for development in isolation, without the input of others. It's important to take a step back and to consider with honesty who you are as a professional. Think about who is in a position to help you do this; perhaps a colleague or a friend who knows how you work. Seek their advice when planning and goal-setting, and set time aside for this. Don't expect to be able to achieve a sensible plan for the future on an ad hoc basis, but do remember that your success in personal and professional development is yours to define.

Creating a plan

Use this framework of questions to help you focus your thoughts on your development needs and formulate a plan for the future. This is not an exhaustive list by any means, but you may like to consider whether you feel inspired or hindered by the questions. Use them to help you to identify the direction you'd like to take and the goals you'd like to reach.

As you work through the questions in Table 7.1, think about these points:

- Trust your instincts and intuitive feelings when deciding where you want to go in your career and the path you'd like to take to get there. What do your gut feelings tell you?
- Do you want to focus on expanding existing skills or pursuing the development of new skills? A combination of the two is probably a wise balance to aim for.
- Gather as much information as possible on any funding that may be available to you on a national, local or school-based level.
- Think about whether you'd like a professional mentor. Who might this be?
- Make your plans in terms of short-, medium- and long-term goals and be sure to define to yourself what you mean by this. Make sure that your goals are SMART – that is, specific, measurable, achievable, relevant and time-related. Your goals need to take into account:

  - your job description and what your role has become (if different)
  - the aims of your department or curriculum area
  - your school's development plan
  - your learning style
  - your values

- Aim to distinguish between what you feel to be urgent (and why) and what you consider to be important (and why). Don't rely on any objectives that have been selected as a result of the performance management process as this is not a replacement for a strategic career development plan.
- Aim to align yourself to your work through your strategic planning. Its purpose is to support your needs.
- Be aware of any gender-based values that may be influencing your plan. What is motivating you?
- Remember that a simple makeover of some aspect of your work can revitalise your approach to your job. Be open to the opportunities you may have to 'tweak' and imaginative about how this can help you.

Table 7.1

Strengths	Development needs	Opportunities	Limitations
What is positive about my current work situation?	What is negative about my current work situation?	What aspects of my current work situation can I use to my advantage?	What limits me in my current work situation?
What are my skills and areas of expertise?	What are the gaps in my skills base?	Are there opportunities to fill gaps in my skills base in my current school?	Are there any valid reasons not to develop my skills base being presented to me?
What specialist knowledge do I have?	What specialist knowledge would I like to have?	What professional development would provide me with the specialist knowledge I want?	What are the blocks to my gaining specialist knowledge?
What are my existing qualifications?	Are there any qualifications I could be working towards?	Is there a way of achieving the qualifications I want while remaining in post?	Do my circumstances allow for the time to pursue additional qualifications?
What are the positive aspects of my character and personality?	Do any aspects of my personality and character have a negative impact on my work?	Can I utilise my personality and characteristics to further my own and others' professional development?	Is my personality inhibited in any way in my present circumstances?
How do my personal values affect my work?	Do I consider personal values when at work?	Is there a way in which I can incorporate my personal values in my work?	Does my school's ethos (both real and imagined) conflict with my personal values?
What circumstances best support my success?	Is there anything I can do to encourage the circumstances that best support my success?	Can I take advantage of any national professional development initiatives?	Does my current post support me or limit me?
What is the most valuable contribution I have made during my career?	Am I contributing to my school's environment as effectively as I could be?	What opportunities do I have to contribute further?	Are my attempts to have a greater impact on my school blocked in any way?

ACTION Where do you want your career to take you?

Why have you reached this conclusion?

Who can help you to achieve your goals?

Where can you get the information you need?

What moves you in your work – *really* moves you?

How is this reflected in your career plan?

Are you willing and/or able to invest any of your own money in your career development?

Do you consider that your age has an impact on your goals and motivations?

Have you readily identified your daily learning opportunities? How do these feature in your plan?

Are you open to the 'domino effect' – the fact that one thing usually leads to another, often unseen opportunity?

Can you view your plan within the greater context of your life's experiences?

ABOUT CAREER PLANNING FOR NEWLY QUALIFIED TEACHERS

To a certain extent, newly qualified teachers in England are at a distinct advantage when it comes to career planning and thinking about professional development. For a start, they have the Career Entry and Development Profile (CEDP) – a document designed to help new teachers think about their development at key stages of their training and induction.

The CEDP helps new teachers to make constructive connections between initial teacher training, induction and continuing development. It seeks to focus reflection on achievements and goals as well as nurturing the need for collaborative discussion between new teachers and their more experienced colleagues.

Just as all thinking about professional and personal development should, the CEDP encourages an emphasis on *process* as opposed to box-ticking. It seeks to assist teachers in identifying their skills and abilities as well as their development needs and achieves this best through continuing collaborative processes.

New teachers have to use the CEDP, but could also usefully keep in mind the ideas discussed in this chapter whenever time allows.

For a copy of the CEDP visit: www.tta.gov.uk or call the publications line on: 0845 6060 323.

Career satisfaction

There is little value in pursuing a career in which you cannot feel dynamic and gain a solid return by way of job satisfaction. Your personal and professional development is not just about the improvement of your teaching and your pupils' learning. It is also about anchoring your need for nourishment from your career in a tangible strategic plan that can take you to the places you want to go and give you the experiences you crave. People talk about getting a 'buzz' from certain activities, and indeed need that buzz in order to enhance their life's experiences. Committing ourselves to ongoing professional development is one way in which we can be sure to pepper our working life with bubbles of excitement and even 'buzzing' periods.

Other factors which can contribute to our sense of career satisfaction and well-being include:

- the extent to which we feel we are rewarded appropriately for our work
- the extent to which we feel adequately trained and qualified to perform our role; and then executing that role according to the training we receive
- creating our own methods for performing the tasks we must complete
- the opportunity to develop on a personal as well as professional level
- being offered ongoing reviews of progress
- participating in ongoing self-review
- selecting roles that match our character and mentality and being aware of the fact that what once suited us may now be hindering us

Career satisfaction is rarely to be found in working harder at your job. Cliché it may be, but it's worth repeating as often as possible: Work smarter, not harder. It's a worthy goal to pursue!

There are no ordinary moments in working life. Allow yourself to recognise your achievements on a day-to-day basis and just spare a thought for how far you are travelling in terms of your personal and professional development. This is what will give you the impetus to continue always learning, growing and developing. Your career is a series of extraordinary moments!

- Ally yourself with like-minded colleagues. Link with like-minded teachers from other schools whenever possible. Internet staffroom forums such as that found at www.eteach.com are excellent for this.

- Network whenever you can. Take the names and numbers of teachers you meet on courses or at meetings. Be free in your exchange of information and open to what opportunities may be there for you. Have you met someone who can help you to achieve your goals? Never miss an opportunity!
- Work at building relationships with colleagues. Co-operate whenever you can and work collectively as well as individually.
- Give as well as receive during the course of your work.

ACTION How important is career satisfaction to your sense of well-being?

How much satisfaction does your career offer you?

Is there anything within your power that you can do to support your levels of satisfaction?

Is there anything that others in your circle can do to support your levels of satisfaction?

Can you develop networks with other schools in your area to help you to enhance your sense of career well-being?

Key sources of information

For a round-up of the current national picture of continuing professional development for teachers, visit:

- England: www.teachernet.gov.uk/professionaldevelopment
- Wales: www.learning.wales.gov.uk
- Scotland: www.ltscotland.org.uk
- Northern Ireland: www.deni.gov.uk

The UK General Teaching Councils also carry information on continuing professional development:

- England: www.gtce.org.uk
- Wales: www.gtcw.org.uk
- Scotland: www.gtcs.org.uk
- Northern Ireland: www.gtcni.org.uk

Your local education authority will also have information on local professional learning opportunities, and most independent companies offering courses will target schools direct.

ABOUT ONLINE INTERACTIVE PROFESSIONAL DEVELOPMENT COURSES

The Internet is one area where opportunities for professional learning abound. Companies such as Fieldwork Online Training provide good-value courses for school staff of all levels. These are simple to use and offer teachers maximum flexibility. Schools rather than individual teachers subscribe to the courses, and the aim is that anyone doing the courses then has complete control over when they do a course and how long it takes them. Although all courses offer a certificate of achievement, it is possible for these to contribute to further professional learning at masters level.

For more information on online interactive professional development, visit: www.fieldworkonlinetraining.com

CHAPTER 8

Well-being and life – the wider picture

Perhaps the greatest art that we can ever master in our lives is to *balance* our lives. Well-being at work is just part of the story. The sub-plot has to be focus on the wider picture of well-being and life in general.

We are never *just* teachers. All of us are, or have been, sons or daughters, and some of us are also parents, grandparents, husbands, wives, partners, brothers, sisters, and so on. We may also have other roles in life such as volunteering for a charity or being a member of a sports team. Teaching, although a significant part of life, is not the be-all and end-all of who we are.

If we do not take the time to care for our sense of well-being outside school, our ability to function effectively as a teacher will necessarily be much diminished.

The topics covered in this chapter emerged from the requests of teachers during the research for this book. Although the threats to well-being that come from our wider experience of life beyond the classroom are broad in scope, the following concerns came up in discussions with teachers time and again.

Well-being and nutrition

From treating scurvy with vitamin C to diving for fatty and sugary foods when we're feeling low, humans have long known and respected the impact that food and nutrition can have on physical and mental well-being. Many nutrition experts have written on the particular nutritional needs of different professions. The following advice comes from the Institute for Optimum Nutrition and is included as information only. It is advisable to seek the support of a qualified nutritional therapist if you are planning to alter significantly your food and supplement intake. Further information can be found at www.ion.ac.uk

Taking supplements for energy

Patrick Holford, founder of the Institute for Optimum Nutrition, suggests that the following supplements should be taken to maximise energy levels. It looks like a frighteningly long list, but these optimal levels can be achieved by taking a high-strength multivitamin and multimineral, rather than separate pills for each vitamin and mineral.

- B1 (thiamine)   25–100 mg
- B2 (riboflavin)   25–100 mg
- B3 (niacin)   50–150 mg
- B5 (pantothenic acid)   50–200 mg
- B6 (pyridoxine)   50–100 mg
- B12 (cyanocobalamin)   10–100 mcg
- folic acid   100–400 mcg
- biotin   50–150 mcg
- co-enzyme Q10   10–90 mg
- vitamin C   1000–3000 mg
- calcium   150–500 mg
- magnesium   100–1000 mg
- iron   5–15 mg
- zinc   10–20 mg
- chromium   100–300 mcg

Nutrition for energy

Certain foods will help you to maintain optimal energy levels. The following foods are suggested:

- foods rich in B vitamins (for example, fresh fruit, raw vegetables, wheat-germ, seeds, nuts, wholegrains, meat, fish, eggs and dairy produce, although these levels are reduced when the food is cooked or stored for a long time)

- foods rich in Vitamin C (for example, peppers, watercress, cabbage, broccoli, cauliflower, strawberries, lemons, kiwi fruit, oranges and tomatoes)
- foods rich in magnesium (for example, wheatgerm, almond, cashew nuts, buckwheat and green vegetables)
- foods rich in calcium (for example, cheese, almonds, green vegetables, seeds and prunes)
- foods rich in zinc (for example, oysters, lamb, nuts, fish, egg yolk, wholegrains and almonds)
- foods rich in iron (for example, pumpkin seeds, almonds, cashew nuts, raisins and pork)
- foods rich in Co Q10 (for example, all meat and fish, especially sardines, eggs, spinach, brocolli, alfalfa, potato, soya beans and soya oil, wheat, especially wheatgerm, rice, bran, buckwheat, millet and most beans, nuts and seeds)
- foods rich in chromium (for example, whole foods such as wheatflour, bread and pasta, beans, nuts and seeds, asparagus and mushrooms)

Nutrition to help combat negative stress

The adrenal glands produce cortisol, adrenaline, noradrenaline and DHEA (hormones). When we're under prolonged negative stress we can struggle to produce adequate amounts of these 'motivating molecules'. To help combat this the body needs:

- essential fats such as starflower oil (1000 mg a day) or evening primrose oil (four 500 mg supplements a day)
- vitamin B6 (100 mg)
- zinc (20 mg)
- magnesium (300 mg)

Do also eat little and often through particularly stressful periods.

Calming foods

Just like certain moods can have us reaching for our latest craving, the foods we eat can affect our mood, too. There has been plenty of research into food and mood such that we now know the kinds of food we can use to help us to move towards a feeling of calm.

In her book *101 Ways to Simplify Your Life* (see Further Reading), Susannah Olivier suggests that the following twenty foods can have a calming effect:

- Protein foods such as legumes (including peas, beans, lentils, soybeans and alfalfa), nuts, cheese, fish and meat are sources of tryptophan, which is a calming brain chemical. Eating a little protein with each meal can help to prevent mood swings.
- Oats are a 'classic relaxation food'. As a whole grain they help to balance blood sugar and as a carbohydrate help the brain to process tryptophan.
- Calcium has calming properties. Milk is rich in calcium but it is best absorbed from skimmed milk. If you cannot tolerate dairy produce, it is possible to buy calcium-enriched soya milk or rice milk.
- Basil is thought to be a 'highly calming food' which can even help to induce sleepiness.
- Calming teas or tisanes can be a good alternative to tea and coffee, even if you are already used to taking the decaffeinated versions. Particularly soothing options include camomile, lemon balm and lavender.
- Molasses can be a useful sugar substitute. It's high in calcium and magnesium that balance the nervous system and, used in small quantities, won't cause the blood-sugar swings that refined sugar can.
- Other sugar substitutes include honey (manuka honey is highest in compounds that fight infection), dried fruit (high in magnesium and iron) and sweet fruits such as bananas (high in nerve-balancing potassium).
- Chocolate makes us feel better as it appears to trigger the same brain chemicals that are released when we are in love. A high-quality chocolate with 60–70 per cent cocoa solids eaten in moderation is ideal.
- Orange juice with sparkling water can give a vitality kick.
- Selenium helps to maintain mood balance. Brazil nuts are rich in this mineral, as are rice, wheat, seaweed and seafood, especially shrimp and tuna.

- Fish oils have been shown to alleviate depression and hyperactivity.
- Magnesium-rich foods are vital to help calm the mind and balance moods. Green leafy vegetables are rich in magnesium, as are dried fruit, nuts, seeds and legumes.
- The combination of pear, ginger and celery is thought to be a good mood-booster – pear for its potassium content, celery as a nerve tonic and ginger for a pick-me-up. To make this juice, put one pear, one or two celery sticks and a 2.5 cm cube of ginger in a juicer.
- Certain herbs are thought to provide an antidote to tension headaches. Steep in boiling water for 10 minutes 1.5 teaspoons of mixed dried skullcap, lavender flowers and lemon verbena. Strain and sweeten with honey if required.
- The B-vitamins and vitamin C help to calm the nervous system.
- Lettuce is thought to aid relaxation.
- All fruits and vegetables are rich in antioxidants which help to prevent age-related brain degeneration. Eat at least five portions a day.
- Mint is thought to help to lower feelings of anger and nervousness. Add it to salads and vegetables.
- Zinc and iron are essential for optimum brain function, mental health and mood balance. Good sources are lean meats, seafood, nuts, seeds, whole grains and legumes.

Remember to make any changes to your diet slowly. Being mindful of what you eat and the potential impact it can have on your overall well-being is not about fanaticism or hard and fast rules. It's about common sense and listening to your body.

Boosting immunity

We can have a rather strange attitude towards illness and disease or 'disease'. We think that when it strikes it does so out of the blue, yet the symptoms we experience are simply evidence that our bodies are fighting to rebalance themselves.

Your body is your last line of defence that all is not well. Physical, mental and emotional symptoms manifest themselves because they are the loudest signal we are likely to hear. We owe it to ourselves to listen to our body.

Frequent coughs, colds, sore throats, allergies and even persistent tired-ness are all signs of an immune system under pressure. Listen to your body's needs. There are valid reasons for feeling tired; most cell repair takes place when we sleep, so if we ignore the feelings of fatigue and a need to snooze we are preventing these essential repairs from taking place.

Mind over matter?

We know that there is a link between mind and body, but can this go as far as affecting immunity? Studies in the past have found a link between the brain and the immune system. It seems that the two speak the same chemical language. The mind can turn down the immune response, and conditioning can improve it, and tools such as relaxation and visualisation are known to have an impact on preventing and 'treating' disease as well as improving quality of life.

Immunity action

Your natural immunity is your best weapon in the fight against 'dis-ease'. When you consider the number of people you interact with on a daily basis, and that each one of these carries a different cocktail of bugs and germs, a healthy immune system is essential.

Regardless of where your allegiances lie when it comes to healthcare, what is certain is that we should not be dismissive of allopathic (or con-ventional) medicine or of complementary medicine. This is particularly important when taking steps to boost your levels of immunity.

These steps can help in keeping you physically healthy:

- Increase your intake of antioxidants, which help to boost your immunity. Vitamin A strengthens cells that keep viruses at bay, and vitamin C will fight any that do get through. Zinc helps immune cells to mature, and selenium helps them to identify invaders. Eat more apples, oranges, red, green and yellow vegetables, carrots, potatoes, grains, seeds, nuts and cereals.
- Take an immunity-boosting supplement such as Echinacea, aloe vera, garlic or bee pollen. Your local healthfood stockist (be sure to go to a specialist store rather than to a supermarket) will help you identify which one is most suitable for you.

- Keep your lungs healthy by exercising, singing, or playing a wind instrument.
- Devote time to exercise. This will greatly support your lymphatic system, which is essential to eliminating toxins from the body.

ABOUT FIGHTING COLDS

Most staffrooms will have at least one teacher battling the symptoms of a cold. Trying to muster the energy to teach through a cold is virtually impossible, so consider taking these steps at the first sneeze or snivel:

- Take a high dose of vitamin C (one gram three times a day). Vitamins A and B-complex will help, too.
- Suck a zinc lozenge. Zinc is thought to reduce the time you are sick with a cold.
- Eat lightly and drink plenty of water, even more than usual, as this helps to wash out toxins.
- Use eucalyptus essential oil dabbed on to a tissue to help to clear sinuses.
- Rest as much as possible, especially in the early stages of a cold.

For further information on boosting immunity, look at Further Reading.

Most folks are about as happy as they make up their minds to be.
(Abraham Lincoln)

Within you there is a stillness and a sanctuary to which you can retreat and be yourself.

(Hermann Hesse)

The principle of life is that life responds by corresponding; your life becomes the things you have decided it shall be.

(Raymond Charles Barker)

ABOUT 'LEISURE SICKNESS'

Researchers in the Netherlands coined the phrase 'leisure sickness' to describe the phenomenon of falling ill on the first day of a holiday. Apparently around 3 per cent of us do it, but this figure is likely to be higher among teaching professionals. A heavy workload, perfectionist tendencies and a strong sense of responsibility all contribute to the causes of holiday illness. Perhaps the reason for this is that we put illness off until we have time for it! The minute we're able to relax we succumb to whatever we've been harbouring from the previous term.

Avoiding 'leisure sickness' or the 'Saturday migraine' is easy. All you need to do is take care of your well-being on an ongoing basis. Be observant of symptoms and never deny them. Take a day if you need it and make sure your next opportunity to relax is always in sight.

ABOUT DEEP VEIN THROMBOSIS

There have been press reports about how deep vein thrombosis, or DVT, can affect those who sit for long periods without moving their legs. Typically this appears to happen (to those who are susceptible) on long journeys such as long-haul flights, but it can happen as a result of, for example, sitting at a desk for hours without walking around.

DVT is relatively uncommon, but when it does strike it can kill. If you're tackling a mountain of marking or paperwork, do yourself a favour and be certain to get up and walk around at least once every half-hour. Run up and down the stairs or do a few gentle stretches to get your circulation going.

The signs to watch out for are swelling, pain, tenderness or redness particularly if this is at the back of the leg below the knee. Seek immediate medical attention.

Exercise

Love it or hate it, your body *needs* it! Exercise, particularly aerobic exercise, gets oxygen moving round your body, gives your heart and other muscles a full workout and makes your brain feel refreshed.

There really is no choice over whether you're active or not. What you have choice over is which type of activity you go for. From inexpensive or free activities such as swimming, running or jogging and walking to the more expensive end of the spectrum such as joining a gym or playing a team or competitive sport that might require equipment, there is a tremendous range to choose from.

These ideas may help you in that choice:

- Go for a sport that does not compromise your sense of safety. For example, jogging alone is not going to make you feel comfortable through the winter months if you're nervous of being out in the dark.
- Exercise with friends if you think that they'll keep you motivated.
- Drink water at regular intervals through any exercise that you do.
- Give yourself goals and targets to go for.
- Make the time for exercise. Saying that you couldn't possibly fit it in is not a valid excuse. Exercise is an essential part of your road to well-being, so commit yourself to it now!
- Vary the exercise that you do. Don't get into the same old routines as your body will get decreasing benefits from the time spent on it.
- Listen to your body. Don't force it on a run when it really wants a gentle swim, and don't stifle its need to exert energy when your mind says 'Let's slump in front of the TV'!
- In his book *Waterlog* (see Further Reading), Roger Deakin refers to walking, swimming and cycling as 'subversive activities' because they allow us to break free from an official version of things. They are also free, or inexpensive, and can be interpreted in the way that suits us best at the time. Are there any physical activities that create that feeling in you?
- The British Trust for Conservation Volunteers is involved in the Green Gym, which is a scheme designed to improve health and fitness while taking part in conservation activities. Visit www.greengym.org.uk for further information, or find out from your local conservation groups if a similar scheme is running near where you live.

Walking as fitness

The good news for time-poor teachers is that one of the most effective forms of exercise is walking. Researchers have described it as 'the nearest activity to perfect exercise', not to mention the fact that it's free!

There are numerous benefits to be had from increasing the amount of walking you do in your day-to-day life. These include, among many others:

- toning and strengthening muscles
- increasing endurance
- boosting immunity
- improving cardiovascular fitness
- reducing the impact of negative stress
- maintaining a healthy weight
- improving sleep patterns
- improving energy levels

If you're considering walking more as a form of fitness, consider these points:

- Make a commitment to yourself. Aim to go out for a fitness walk a certain number of times a week. Even if you aim for just one outing a week, that will offer benefits. The important thing is not the number of walks you do, but the act of commitment to it each week.
- Aim for a pace of between 12–20 minutes per mile (8–12 minutes per kilometre).
- Make sure your footwear is supportive and clothing is comfortable.
- Pay attention to your posture when walking. No slouching!
- Breathe deeply, using your diaphragm.
- Keep your personal safety in mind. Don't walk alone at night unless you tell someone your route and take sensible safety precautions such as ensuring you can be seen and carrying a mobile phone with you if you have one. Never use a personal stereo when walking out alone.
- Take the opportunity to do a bit of positive thinking. According to researchers in the USA, those who think positively, particularly about ageing, live seven and a half years longer than those who don't.
- Remember, it doesn't need to be a long walk. You'll lose the benefits if you end up feeling stressed about the time you've just spent walking!

For further information on walking as exercise, try *Walking for Fitness* by Nina Barough (see Further Reading).

EXAMPLE AN EVENING WALK

My boyfriend and I decided that we would go for a walk every evening, whatever the weather. He's a teacher as well, so it was really easy for us both to get in from work, have a quick cup of tea and immediately start working again, stopping to have a bite to eat at about 8 p.m. We realised that our evenings were non-existent and we were both sluggish and tired all the time. So we decide before we leave how long we want to walk. If it's, say, half an hour, we walk in any direction for fifteen minutes and then turn round and walk back again. Sometimes we stay in the town, other times we head out towards the country, but we get out walking every day after school. It's been great for our relationship and for our fitness and energy levels. If someone had tried to convince me it would make that much difference, I would never have believed them!

(Secondary teacher with five years' experience)

High blood pressure

If a doctor or other healthcare provider has told you that your blood pressure needs lowering, you owe it to yourself to take every step you can to support any treatment you may be receiving. While there's no magic bullet to reduce high blood pressure, there are plenty of measures that can help.

Untreated, high blood pressure, or hypertension, can lead to heart disease, kidney damage, blindness, heart attack and stroke among others.

Statistics show that people with hypertension are:

- six times more likely to develop congestive heart failure
- three times more likely to develop coronary heart disease
- seven times more likely to have a stroke

If you have been diagnosed with high blood pressure, remember that you are not alone; around 10 million people in the UK have it. And this is not just an issue for men. Heart disease is reportedly the top killer of women over 55.

There are several known risk factors, including:

- Diet. High sodium intake is thought to raise blood pressure. Processed foods contain high levels of salt.
- Alcohol. Epidemiological studies have shown that more than three to five drinks a day have a distinct impact on increasing the risk of heart disease.
- Lack of exercise. The American Heart Association says that those who don't exercise are up to 52 per cent more likely to develop high blood pressure than those who do exercise.
- Negative stress. Emotions such as anger, depression and fear all have the potential to raise blood pressure.
- Smoking. The constriction that nicotine causes in blood vessels places additional pressure on the heart and raises blood pressure over time.

A detailed programme and guidance in lowering blood pressure can be found in S T and J Sinatra's *Lower Your Blood Pressure in 8 Weeks* (see Further Reading).

Sleep

One of the most common causes of insomnia is stress; yet, ironically, it is when we are under perceived stress that the restful state of unconsciousness that sleep offers is most needed. Not only does sleep refresh us for a new day; when the body is asleep cell damage is repaired and immune function is at its most active.

Increased health niggles, such as colds and coughs, seem to be an inevitable consequence of lack of sleep, which in turn affects day-to-day functioning. On top of this, when tiredness takes hold, everything seems so personal; every comment heard can feel like a put-down, and it can seem that the rational mind has gone absent without leave! So much of our well-being hinges on good-quality uninterrupted sleep.

If sleep can be a problem for you, consider these points:

- Camomile tea before bed to ward off insomnia may be a bit of an old folk remedy, but there are many who would not go to bed without it. Studies have shown that camomile contains compounds with calming actions.

- Research has shown that herb Kava Kava could relieve stress-induced insomnia.
- Caffeine is often consumed in greater quantities when under stress, but its adrenaline-mimicking qualities lead to an increase in nervous tension, thus exacerbating the problem. Opt for caffeine-free drinks where possible, but if you have a long history of caffeine consumption do not expect to reduce consumption without withdrawal symptoms. Caffeine is addictive, so cutting back slowly is the wisest way.

ABOUT PROGRESSIVE MUSCLE RELAXATION

This is a simple way of relaxing your muscles.

Lie down in a comfortable place where you won't be disturbed. Close your eyes and, working from the top down, tense the muscles in your face for 8–10 seconds (or until it starts to feel uncomfortable) and then relax, letting them go. Move down to your neck and do the same thing. Repeat the exercise with the different muscle groups in your body, chest, stomach, buttocks, arms, hands and so on.

This works well because when tension is created and then released muscles have no choice but to relax; and in fact, if you lie still, the level of relaxation reached is likely to be deeper than before you introduced tension. As you relax your muscles, notice how your breathing slows and deepens. Your heart rate and blood pressure will fall, too, and you may start to feel mentally calm.

The more often you do this the more adept you will be.

- Take time to unwind before going to bed, even if only for fifteen minutes. Working late simply borrows time from the next day. Avoid news programmes at this time (even try a 'news fast').
- Aim to regulate your bedtime so that your body gets into the habit of sleep. Go for more hours of sleep before midnight, as these are thought to be most beneficial for us.
- Do not spend hours in bed being unable to sleep. Try getting up (but resist the urge to work) and perhaps do some light reading to induce sleep.
- Take a good look round your bedroom. Is it a purely restful room, free of clutter and 'jobs', or could it use some attention? De-junk your

bedroom as much as possible and create a space of calm tranquillity. We spend around a third of our lives asleep, so it's worth investing in the best mattress you can possibly afford.

- Always seek the advice of your chosen healthcare provider if sleeplessness becomes a habit.

ABOUT NATURAL SLEEP REMEDIES

Your chosen healthcare provider will be able to help you decide if any insomnia you are suffering may need chemical treatment, but you might want to consider the following natural remedies that have been shown to induce sleep. In her book *Sleep: A natural guide* (see Further Reading), Belinda Grant Viagas recommends these remedies among others. Raw ingredients will be available from a good-quality healthfood store:

- Passiflora tincture. Take these drops about 30 minutes before bedtime.
- Hops tea. Steep three hop heads in a mug of boiling water for 3–5 minutes (some people are allergic to hops, so take care if you have never tried this before).
- Put half an ounce of valerian in a glass of cold water for twenty-four hours and take one tablespoon of the liquid three hours before bed.
- Bach Flower Remedies such as Mimulus, Rock Rose, Hornbeam, Heather, Holly, Chicory and Willow can all be useful for sleep disorders. A qualified practitioner will be able to help you to decide which one is best for you.
- Tissue salts such as Calc. Phos., Ferr. Phos., Kali. Phos. and Mag. Phos. all have their uses for inducing sleep. Again, a qualified homeopath will be able to prescribe the best one for you.

An optimist expects his dreams to come true; a pessimist expects his nightmares to.

(Hermann Hesse)

> ## EXAMPLE ATTACKING INSOMNIA
>
> My doctor told me about getting as many hours of sleep before midnight as possible, and I thought he was mad. I found it hard to get to sleep much before 2 a.m. and then I was always up at about five. But it does take discipline. I was determined to break the habits I was in. I didn't really take anything, but I did cut out caffeine and made sure I was actually in bed by 10 p.m. and no later. I didn't watch TV or listen to the radio or talk to my partner. It took about two weeks of being determined, and eventually I was falling asleep earlier and earlier. For me, it really works. I've never had so much energy, but I really feel it if I go to bed too late.
>
> (Primary NQT)

Affirmations

Words like 'serenity', 'peace', 'tranquillity', 'calm' and so on can actually have an effect on the mind of the burned out and blue. Repeating them to yourself with frequency is thought to start to train your mind to experience the feeling described.

If you think you might be susceptible to this kind of conditioning, consider using affirmations. An affirmation is an often-repeated phrase that focuses on something positive. They are an excellent way of managing negativity, but there are some important points to remember when constructing them:

- Always use positive statements. Say 'My work is enjoyable and manageable' rather than 'I am not stressed about my work'.
- Use present rather than future statements. 'I am calm and relaxed' is better than 'I will be calm and relaxed'.
- Visualise your ideal scenario while you use affirmations. Believe that you can create the situations you want to create.
- Repeat your affirmations often throughout the day. Research suggests that the mind needs to hear an affirmation at least six times before positive benefits can be achieved.

ACTION If you feel as though your heart is racing, and you are in a position to lie down on your side, listen to the speed of its beating. Then, taking long, deep breaths, quietly repeat the words 'slow' and 'calm'. Can you *hear* a difference in your heart rate? Is it beating more slowly at your suggestion?

Your leisure time

It's not unfair to say that many of us can at times feel uncomfortable with leisure time. We are so used to working life encroaching on our so-called home life that any leisure time we may manage to ring-fence can be frittered away. It's easier to work, with its rhythms, deadlines, bells, goals, routines and rules, than it is creatively to use the time when we don't work.

Thinkers on leisure have pointed to the fact that pursuing hobbies demands time and discipline if they are to be experienced as *'re-creation'*. As a result, the leisure industry has tended to be built around observing the achievements of others, whether in the field of sport or the arts for example, rather than taking part ourselves. It's a poor substitute for recreational leisure.

ABOUT HOLI-DAYS

A 'holi-day' is a day on which you actively create that 'holiday feeling'. It's not so much about what you do to pass the time during the day as about the feeling you have about it. Even the smallest of activities can send nurturing signals to your mind such as taking an extra long time over your ablutions, going shopping and treating yourself to something you don't 'need', meeting a friend for lunch, chilling out in the pub, playing with your children, going to a gig you've looked forward to, and so on. Don't miss opportunities to create that holiday feeling around apparently day-to-day activities. Just remember, these days are for you and those with whom you want to spend them. They should never be used to catch up with schoolwork.

When planning how to spend your leisure time, consider these points:

- Arrange 'dates' whenever you can. Booking theatre or cinema tickets, or committing yourself to attend a club or a class, or take part in a team sport will ensure that you are at a particular place at a certain time. Fix these 'dates' in your mind; they're not to be cancelled at the last minute.
- Be aware of any changes in your efficiency when you know you have a limited time to achieve something. If you are going out at 7.30 p.m. to pursue a leisure activity, you simply have to get what you need to do done by the time you leave.

ACTION Complete the following sentences making sure that your responses are all leisure-related:

If there's one thing I do today it's . . .
If there's one thing I do this week it's . . .
If there's one thing I do this month it's . . .
If there's one thing I do this year it's . . .
If there's one thing I do this decade it's . . .

Now make the commitment to yourself that you will achieve these goals!

- Be in control of your leisure time. What do you really want to do with it? Do you watch television out of habit or because you love it and know that it enhances your well-being? How else do you typically spend your valuable time off? Would you make changes to these choices if you could?
- Be observant of how your leisure time makes you feel. Does it energise you or make you feel inadequate? Do you beat yourself up over wasting it or feel that you are in control of utilising it effectively?

ACTION Think of something, within reason, that you have always wanted to do that is not work-related (make sure it's realistic and affordable). Make a plan to fulfil this dream in the very near future and take steps *today* to achieve this.

- Think about how you apportion your time. Do you ever get 'self time'? Or is it a matter of grabbing whatever is left at the end of a day or a week? Is self time even important to you? Perhaps an ideal in life would be for all our time to be considered as self time. At least then all the time we spend at work, with family and friends and in our own company would feel like our own time. A vital ingredient in making your vocation your vacation.

ABOUT YOUR QUALITY OF LIFE

What do you find enjoyable and pleasurable? Think about the question in its broadest sense. For example, the *process* of marking a class set of books when you're up against a time limit may not be particularly enjoyable, but the outcome, having completed the task, will certainly give pleasure. The act of abseiling is not exactly enjoyable at the time but the feeling of having done it is certainly pleasurable.

Can you add to your quality of life by recognising when you can derive pleasure from seemingly unenjoyable tasks? If there's any vacant drudgery in your life, how can this be transformed if it cannot be removed?

ACTION Employees at the Eden Project in England are apparently contracted to do things outside their usual zone of comfort to enhance their sense of well-being and creativity, to extend their horizons, and so on. This might include seeing a film or a play they wouldn't normally see or reading a book they wouldn't normally be attracted to.

What can you do like this in the near future to extend your comfort zone?

How does it make you feel?

Feeding your sense of spiritual well-being

For some, keeping an eye on their sense of spiritual well-being is second nature. Habits of contemplation from childhood, whether alone or as part of a congregation for example, spill over into adult life and are maintained with ease. For others, the need to attend to the spirit develops with increasing intensity over time and in response to life's experiences. The problem that then arises centres on how to meet those needs. The soul may need feeding, but on what?

You may belong to a religion, group or organisation which serves your need for a philosophical life-view or for ritual. If you don't, these ideas may help to support your sense of spiritual well-being. They are not in any particular order and are included simply to help trigger your own specific and appropriate solutions.

- Offering thanks is a central theme for many religions. What are you grateful for? Aim to encompass your whole life and include people, places, objects, possessions, opportunities, and so on. Write your list down and view it and revise it regularly.
- Look at the place where you live and work through fresh eyes, as if for the first time. What do you notice? Do you feel naturally at home here? What would improve your sense of well-being here? How would you describe your immediate environment? Does it make you feel energised or drained?
- Are there any places close to you that are known for their spiritual significance? Perhaps there are churches, wells, sacred sites or simply beaches, mountains, moors or downland, and so on, that local people go to for spiritual fulfilment. Do you do the same? Is there somewhere that can do this for you?

EXAMPLE

I do go to church whenever I have the time but I always like to get up onto the [North] Downs, too. There is a particular walk I do that is just the perfect length to get me into a calmer state of mind. When I start my pace is fast and my mind frantic, but by the time I complete the walk everything feels slower and more relaxed. I am addicted to it, I don't mind admitting that!

(Secondary teacher with three years' experience)

- Think about the tasks you perform that are an essential aspect of your job. In what way do they give your day rhythm? Do they add purpose to your day? Can you find meaning in the small stuff?
- What are your hobbies? Do they enrich your life in a spiritual way?
- How do you spend your holidays? In what ways are they enriching experiences for you?
- Do you observe a 'sabbath', even if you are not religious or subscribed to a particular religion? Does one day of the week have a different feeling for you? What makes it different? Is it the clothes you wear, the activities you take part in, or something less tangible? Could you incorporate ten-minute 'sabbaths' into the other days in the week?
- Consider going on a retreat. Findhorn (www.findhorn.org) is now running teacher retreats, or you may want to arrange one for yourself rather than join a purpose-designed one. Do a search on the Internet for appropriate retreats within reach.

EXAMPLE

I treated myself to a retreat. It was wonderful. I felt nervous about joining others, but I shouldn't have been. There were actually six other teachers there and, although we did talk shop to begin with, we soon got into the swing of what we were supposed to be doing. As far as unwinding and de-stressing go, I don't think you could beat it. More conventional holidays can actually be quite stressful but not this. Right from the start I felt positive about the fact that I was giving myself some quality time. My partner was reluctant for me to go but he liked the results!

(Primary NQT)

- How do you express your creativity outside work? Are you comfortable with the word 'creativity'? What, for you, does it encompass?
- Do you have a favourite book? When was the last time you read it? When was the last time you read any book for pure pleasure? Take a trip to your library or bookshop if you feel it's about time you gave yourself some reading time.
- Seen any good films recently? Has anything moved you to tears or inspired you? What's your favourite film? Why? Is it time you watched it again?

- How does music feature in your life? Dig out your favourite CD and play it now.
- When was the last time you went to an art gallery or museum, or anywhere where you could admire the creativity of others? Do you have a list of places you'd like to visit? Make a plan to visit them.
- Do you have friends or family nearby who have known you for a long time? Do you place any value on that kind of familiarity? What do these people give you in terms of spiritual well-being? Read this Arabian proverb: 'A friend is one to whom one may pour out all the contents of one's heart, chaff and grain together, knowing that the gentlest of hands will take and sift it, keep what is worth keeping, and with a breath of kindness blow the rest away.' Do you have anyone in your life who fits this description? Are you this friend to anyone?
- Do you feel a sense of community? What helps to nurture this feeling in you? What do you contribute to the community in which you live? Does any of this have a spiritual significance for you?

ACTION Patrick Nash, Director of the Teacher Support Network in England, once wrote that 'We cannot address the spiritual needs of children unless we address these needs in teachers, their whole life needs. Without this, initiatives to address children's needs are just spin.' Think about this and consider the extent to which you agree with the sentiment. How important is it to you to look after your spiritual and 'whole life' needs?

ABOUT HAPPINESS

Over two thousand years ago, Aristotle concluded that the core of what men and women pursue is happiness. All other goals are pursued only because they will help us to find and experience happiness, not for their own sake. But happiness cannot just 'happen'. It has to be nurtured and cultivated.

Writing for health

Research has found that writing your thoughts and emotions down can help wounds to heal more quickly. It is thought that the process of doing this helps us to process what has happened.

Journalling

It is never harmful to write your feelings down, providing what you commit to paper is not going to be read by anyone else. You don't have to write with any sense or clarity; a stream of consciousness is all it needs to be, although if you prefer to craft something more sophisticated that's fine! The whole point is that your journal should be private to you, so play with words as much as you like.

Psychologists have identified two dimensions of effective communication: that which is *intra*-personal, in other words internal and therefore free, and *inter*-personal, or external and therefore needing to show awareness of the other person's reality. The whole point of writing or journalling is that it is intra-personal.

These ideas may help further:

- Aim to get into a regular discipline of writing. Keep a notebook by your bed and write down your dreams or conscious thoughts as they arise.
- Write a letter to someone who is causing you grief. Explain why this is and exactly how you feel. Don't, however, send it. This is a way of expressing your emotions privately, so that you feel better able to tackle the situation.
- Think of the writing process as a way of grounding thoughts that trouble you.
- If you are not comfortable with the notion of writing, try drawing or doodling your thoughts.
- Whatever it is that you commit to paper, be it about a child, a colleague, an aspect of your job, a situation in which you found yourself, and so on, make sure that it isn't all tirade. Write at least one positive thing to emerge from it all. Aim to remember a time when you felt different about the situation.

> **EXAMPLE** GETTING IT DOWN ON PAPER
>
> I started jotting my thoughts down every now and then a few years ago, but it's a habit now that I can't break. If I have a bad day, I scribble down why I thought it happened. I don't read it back that often, but when I do I often see key themes running through it. I don't want to use it to problem-solve, but it's a great way of off-loading without boring my husband to death!
>
> (Primary teacher with twelve years' experience)

Depression

There are different types of depression, and a general rule of thumb is that you should always seek the help of a qualified professional if you think you may be suffering. Depression is eminently treatable and, although it does still carry a certain stigma, is actually very common.

An unfortunate by-product of experiencing feelings of depression is that it can reduce your ability to seek the help that you need. Self-confidence can be rocked, and what you thought you knew about yourself can be called into question.

There are many symptoms of depression. The following is a brief list, and is not intended to be definitive:

- wanting to withdraw from society and life
- diminishing interest in work life and home life
- forgetfulness
- loss of concentration
- loneliness and isolation
- physical pains, typically in the neck and back, but could be anywhere in the body
- plummeting self-esteem and self-confidence
- reliance on alcohol and/or recreational drugs
- loss of libido
- overwhelming sadness
- guilt
- thoughts of suicide
- loss of control

If you think that you may be experiencing a form of depression, these ideas will help, but do seek the advice of your healthcare provider, too:

• Although the temptation is to withdraw from friends and family when you are experiencing the symptoms of depression, it is really important that you don't do this. If anything, increase your levels of social interaction as soon as symptoms start to kick in. The broader your social circle, the more likely it is that you'll get valued support when you need it.

ACTION Write a list of everyone you would turn to for advice, perspective, a chat, some TLC, practical help and so on. Who is there for you, should you need to call on them?

• Communicate the way that you are feeling. Don't expect people to be perceptive enough to deduce what's going on with you without expressing yourself.
• Take every opportunity to become involved in group activities, whether this be in your home life or working life.
• Take some time to consider what might be at the root of your feelings of depression.
• Remember that feeling depressed is just that, a feeling. It does not mean that your personality has changed, or that you will feel the same way for the rest of your life. What you are feeling right now is temporary.
• Exercise is a sure way of inducing good feelings. The moment that feelings of depression kick in, increase your level of physical activity, even if you feel tired and lethargic. Something as simple as a walk will help – and if you can do this with someone else, all the better.
• Some foods are thought to help alleviate feelings of depression. Current advice suggests increasing your intake of raw and lightly cooked vegetables and fish, mixed seeds (especially linseeds) and fresh and dried fruit. Go for organic when possible. Avoid refined foods such as additives, sugar, coffee and colas as well as cheese and alcohol.

ABOUT FEELINGS OF SUICIDE

It's common during a bout of depression at least to think about what would happen if you got so low that you felt suicidal. Recognising that suicide may be an end possibility of unresolved depression does not mean that you will actually kill yourself, but it does mean that you must seek professional advice right now.

There are many sources of help for the potentially suicidal. Your health-care provider is an obvious port of call, as are telephone helplines such as the Samaritans and Teacher Support Line. If you are feeling depressed and suicidal as a result of grief, there are specific help groups in every town that your doctor or other healthcare provider will be able to tell you about.

Above all else, never think that you are causing a nuisance with your feelings, or that you should just be able to pull yourself together. There are many people, all over the world, who have felt suicidal, and there are many effective techniques out there that can provide lasting help. You are not alone, but do be sure to listen to your symptoms while they're being whispered to you and not when every cell in your body is screaming for attention.

As Clarissa Pinkola Estés wrote in her book *Women Who Run with the Wolves* (and it's equally applicable to men, too): 'The most important thing is to hold on, hold out, for your creative life, for your solitude, for your time to be and do, for your very life; hold on, for the promise from the wild nature is this: after winter, *spring always comes*.'

Nothing has changed but my attitude. Everything has changed.
(Anthony de Mello)

A hobby puts to work those unused talents which might otherwise become restless, and it provides us with a form of activity in which there is no need whatever to strive for success.
(Hal Falvey)

Many of life's failures are people who did not realise how close they were to success when they gave up.
(Thomas Edison)

EXAMPLE FEELING DEPRESSED

I was diagnosed with reactive depression two years ago. At first I thought it had ruined my life. I had to have five months off school and found myself fighting feelings of hopelessness and helplessness. I wasn't suicidal – I don't think I'd ever do that – but I couldn't understand how I would get through the next day, and my life just seemed to loom ahead of me, decade after decade. My future felt utterly desolate and bleak. It was like falling, falling deep into myself and not even realising that the pit in me was bottomless. But then I did reach 'rock bottom'. I knew I couldn't go any lower. I was having regular counselling and leaned heavily on those around me. There was no way I could work through it. But from the bottom there is only one way to go, and gradually I rebuilt myself again. It was a life-changing experience, and I learned so much. I know exactly what the warning signs are, and that self-knowledge is invaluable. It sounds strange, but I'd recommend depression to anyone!

(Secondary teacher with ten years' experience)

ACTION Imagine your discontent as a contained mass with a root. Where would this root be fixed? In a specific person such as a partner, a past lover, a parent, a colleague or a pupil? In a dimension of your work? In an event from the past? In a fear of the future? Where, specifically? Use this information to target your actions in your pursuit of well-being.

Counselling

There are many different definitions and types of counselling, but, put simply, it is a working relationship in which you are helped to explore and manage what is happening in your life.

The Teacher Support Network in England explains that the overall aim of counselling is to provide an opportunity for you to work towards living in a way that is more satisfying and resourceful for you. Everyone has different needs, so there can be no magic-bullet answers.

If counselling is to work, you need to be fully engaged in the process. That is, you need to be prepared to deal with issues honestly and reflectively. Counselling may be concerned with developmental issues, address-ing and resolving specific problems, making decisions, coping with crises, developing personal insight and knowledge, working through feelings of inner conflict or improving relationships with others. The counsellor's role is to facilitate your work in ways that respect your values, personal resources and capacity for choice within your cultural context.

Counselling is certainly helpful when we want to clarify the problems and challenges facing us, consider the various options open to us and acknowledge the impact of life events on our emotional well-being.

People choose counselling for a variety of reasons, including:

- negative stress in the workplace
- conflict at work or at home
- bereavement
- depression
- loss of confidence, morale or motivation
- poor health (either your own or that of a loved one)

How counselling works

Counselling will be a specific arrangement between you and your coun-sellor and is entirely private. Your counsellor will not make judgements about you and should accept you for who you are.

For effective counselling to take place, you will need to enter into partnership with your counsellor, and to trust and respect him or her. During the process of counselling, your counsellor will clarify and reflect comments back to you so that you can explore further what it is that you are feeling. They will help you to explore fresh perspectives through an interactive two-way process.

It can be just as effective to have telephone or email counselling. Although slightly different processes, both offer a means to reaching work-able solutions for the problematic issues that may be facing you.

What counselling is not

Counselling is not:

- about being a good listener or about needing simply to be listened to
- something that has to last for years, or indefinitely

- psychoanalysis
- about giving and receiving advice
- only for certain types of people

As a client, or participant in counselling:

- You do not have to be ill to benefit from it.
- You do not have to lay yourself open or reveal all your 'secrets'.
- You should not expect your counsellor to solve all the issues and problems in your life.
- You can expect to be helped through the problems you discuss.
- You will probably find you have more energy to solve and deal with the issues facing you.
- You will almost certainly understand the psychological aspects of the situation in greater depth.
- There will be opportunities to explore modifying your behaviour, or that of others, in certain situations.
- You'll be able to discover fresh perspectives, ideas and options.

ACTION Have you ever sought counselling? What was it about the process that helped you most? Can you think of events in your life when you would have benefited from counselling but didn't receive it? Is there anything facing you right now, either in your working life or in your private life, that could be eased by counselling? What steps can you take today to go about seeking the help you need?

Work when there is work to do. Rest when you are tired. One thing done in peace will most likely be better than ten things done in panic. . . . I am not a hero if I deny rest; I am only tired.

(Susan McHenry)

Knowing is not enough; we must apply. Willing is not enough; we must do.

(JW von Goethe)

EXAMPLE FOCUSING ON SOLUTIONS

One of the most striking things about the process of counselling for me was how effectively my counsellor helped me to see that I could work towards solutions. She didn't allow me to wallow at all, and the energy I got from knowing that I was taking decisive, albeit still mental, action was fantastic. I think it's important to trust your counsellor and to have faith in their processes. Some of what she reflected back to me was amazing. I'm happy that I chose counselling as a way of getting over the stuff I was dealing with and I'd definitely do it again. I couldn't get into long-term psychotherapy as I don't think that's for me, but this solution-focused counselling has worked a treat. My only regret is that I didn't discover it earlier!

(Secondary teacher with ten years' experience)

ACTION Think of a problem in your life at present – something you would dearly love to be resolved. Now write a letter to a close friend or a relative. The date is five years from today. Explain in your letter how you resolved the problem and the action that you took. Tell them about the positive outcome and the steps you took to achieve it. What was your 'path of liberation' from that particular problem? Now read back over your letter. What is stopping you from turning this into reality?

Self-respect and self-esteem

So much is made of self-esteem as a cure-all for just about every ailment linked to well-being, or a lack of it, but is that wholly deserved and appropriate? Perhaps self-respect is a more useful concept for teachers. After all, not respecting yourself is a sure but slow suicide. If you're unsure as to the vagaries of the term, Philip Pullman provided a useful definition in his Isis Lecture of April 2003: 'If you want to know the difference, self-respect is the quality that prevents you from talking about your self-esteem'.

In the depths of winter, I finally learned that within me there lay an invincible summer.

(Albert Camus)

ACTION How sharp is your self-respect?

Does it enable you to cope with the challenges in your life?

Does it grant you the right to be happy, to feel worthy and to have your needs met?

Does it allow you to look back on your achievements and feel proud? Can you enjoy the fruits of all your efforts?

Your sense of self-respect cannot be bound in to the views of others. It has to be felt from within. The greater the sense of self-respect that you feel, the more respectfully you'll be able to interact with the world. Just remember that every action you take reflects to the world your sense of self-respect. Use it to help you to make supportive and self-nurturing choices and to express and assert your needs through the appropriate channels when necessary.

EXAMPLE RESPECT OF THE SELF

I think it's so important to have self-respect. I worked for five years in a school where I feel it was systematically sucked from me. It wasn't, of course. I know now that I was nothing like as assertive as I should have been and that plenty of great teachers thrived in that school, but it was a huge lesson to me about how self-respect is not something you can ignore. You can't tuck it away and hope that it'll survive without feeding it and giving it some TLC. I made choice after choice that left me feeling that I didn't have any control. I should have listened to my needs. I do now, and it feels great!

(Primary teacher with fifteen years' experience)

Money management

It's not the place of this book to offer financial advice, but to overlook the financial difficulties that some teachers can face in a guide about teacher well-being would be negligent. Money can be tight for teachers, particularly those who have recently completed initial teacher training with student debts to repay as well as those who may be providing the sole income for a young family. Coping with anxieties about money, which often come in at the top of lists of stressors, as well as the day-to-day stresses of the job, can prove to be an excessive burden. These ideas may help:

- Seek financial advice sooner rather than later. As soon as you think that bills and debts may be getting out of hand, get in touch with your union, which will almost certainly offer financial guidance. Teacher Support Line is another source of help (08000 562 561), as is the Citizen's Advice Bureau. The longer you leave it before taking action, the harder the solution will be to find.
- What are your financial priorities? Have you planned for your financial future in the short term and the long term?
- Are you in the habit of saving regularly, even if this is just a small amount each month? Most banks will run regular-saver accounts which allow you to save a set amount each month by direct debit.
- Do you feel in control of the money flowing out of your account? Create a list of all the direct debits and standing orders you have set up and make sure you know the day on which they are deducted from your current account.
- Read your bank statements. Don't trust them to be mistake-free. Check off each item; people who do this as a matter of course often report that it takes less time than they thought it would.
- Make sure that you know how much it costs you to live. This may sound obvious, but when you sit down and calculate how much you spend on food, on petrol, on your mortgage or rent, on insurances, on utilities bills, on entertainment and so on, you may be surprised to see where the bulk of your cash is flowing.
- Budget for known expenditure, for example, when your car insurance is due, your holiday payments are due or even events such as Christmas. If you budget for what you know you'll be spending, unknown expenditure (for example, car or house repairs) may not be so crippling.
- Are you happy with your pension arrangements? Seek the advice of an independent financial adviser if you want to discuss your options.
- Take control of your credit cards if you have them. We apparently average debts of £5,000 each spread over credit cards, store cards and bank loans, and at levels like that debt can rapidly spiral out of control. Make sure you know at any stage just how much money you have, and how much you owe. Consider transferring your credit card debts

to one card. A financial adviser will be able to help you choose the best deal for you; it's worth shopping around.

- Do you know where you want to be financially in five years' time? In ten years' time? Are you working towards goals such as buying a home, saving for children's education or paying off debts?
- If over-spending is a habit for you, take a moment to consider how long the gratification lasts.

The Teacher Support Network offers support to teachers in England and Wales struggling with debt. Visit www.teachersupport.info for further information, or email: moneyadvisor@teachersupport.info

CHAPTER 9

At a glance: the way to well-being

The following quick-reference action guide is intended to offer 'at a glance' guidance when you feel the need to bust stress or simply remind yourself how to work in a more self-nurturing way. Much of this guidance is explained and expanded on in the relevant chapters in this book, should you require more detail.

AT A GLANCE: alternatives to antibiotics

Antibiotics are an essential weapon against disease, but only when used with respect and care. There is a time and a place for them, yet studies repeatedly appear to show that around 70 per cent of antibiotic treatment courses are 'unnecessary' or 'inappropriate'.

- Remember that symptoms aren't all bad. Often they are simply an indication of an internal healing process. For example, mucus helps to rid the body of toxins, and having a temperature indicates that the immune system has kicked up a gear to fight infection (this is because most bacteria and viruses die when heated).
- A sensible diet rich in wholefoods and good-quality fruits and vegetables (organic when possible) will help to guard against nutritional deficiency. This is essential in fighting disease.
- Maintain a healthy bodyweight (neither over- nor under-weight).

- Reduce your intake of polyunsaturated and saturated fats and oils, going for monounsaturated instead (olive oil and omega-3 oils found in certain fish oils and flaxseed and evening primrose oil for example).
- The nutritional deficiencies common in people who have a weakened immune function include: vitamin B6, folate, vitamin B12, selenium and zinc. Talk to a nutritional therapist about whether you need to supplement these in your diet.
- Other vitamins and minerals that can support immune function include: beta-carotene, vitamins C and E, potassium and magnesium, iron and manganese. Again, always seek professional help and avoid self-prescribing.
- Herbal supplements that have been shown to help immune function include: garlic, venus fly trap plant, echinacea, ginseng, licorice, golden-seal, St John's wort and tea-tree oil among others. Expert advice on this is always prudent.
- A hot bath can be used to induce a fever at home and therefore boost immune function. The steam is soothing for upper respiratory tract infections such as colds, too. Take care not to overdo the heat of the water and finish with a cooler shower if possible.
- Acupuncture has also been found to improve immune function.

AT A GLANCE: anger management

- We all experience irritability and anger, but don't all express it in an explosive way. Are you fully aware of how you express your anger? Would your colleagues, friends and family agree with you?
- In order to keep anger in check we need to be able to recognise the triggers and learn when we are nearing our 'last straw'. Calming measures need to be introduced long before this moment arrives.
- When you register feeling anger, always ask yourself: Will this still make me angry in a year's time?
- Are you able to look at the source of your anger in a different light? Can you reframe it and think less rigidly about it? What's a different perspective on it?
- If you habitually experience anger, consider doing a form of physical exercise such as running, kick boxing, or playing squash or tennis.
- Read up about emotional literacy.

- Write your thoughts down in a journal. Aim to dissipate them before confronting others.
- Be aware of the impact that your anger has on other people. You might feel better for getting something off your chest, but have you simply dumped a load of 'stuff' onto someone else to deal with?
- Aim to solve problems through the proper channels. An outward explosion of anger is simply proof that warning signs of anger overload were not heeded. Take calm and decisive action sooner rather than later.
- Don't harbour anger. Let it go and work at rebuilding any relationships that might have been damaged. If this requires you to forgive, do it. None of us is perfect.

AT A GLANCE: being present

- Be mindful of what you are doing. Divided attention leads to tension, so when you are walking aim just to walk, when you are listening aim just to listen, when you are eating aim just to eat, when you are drinking aim just to drink, and so on.
- Some suffering in life is inevitable, but clinging to the past and worrying over the future will not serve you well. Where are you right now? What can you do about it today? Who is there to help you?
- Right now, aim to accept what is happening in your life. That doesn't mean you have to agree with it or want it, like it or love it. But accepting it can help you to deal with it.
- What do you notice around you? Bring yourself right into the present moment by deliberately making five observations of what surrounds you at this moment.

AT A GLANCE: calming the inner critic

- Recognise that some self-talk is essential, but that persistent negativity from within is not helpful.
- As soon as you recognise that your inner critic has kicked in, think of three positive features of yourself and your work that will counteract your self-criticism.

- Aim to determine the circumstances in which your inner critic gets going. What winds it up? When does it give you an easier time? Does it drive you to perform incessantly or is it gentle enough to allow you time off?
- Be aware of whether it is louder in certain circumstances.
- What tames it? Only you can know the answer, and you'll reach it through self-awareness and self-observance.

AT A GLANCE: choosing a complementary practitioner

- Read about the various therapies that exist and make a list of the ones that appeal to you. For example, some people prefer to be treated while remaining fully dressed, so might perhaps opt for something like homeopathy or reflexology; while others might feel happy about removing clothes for a treatment, so may have a massage or acupuncture. Even though some therapies are evidently more effective in the treatment of certain conditions (for example, acupuncture has an established track record in reducing pain), your sense of personal comfort has to be taken into consideration.
- Look for local practitioners in the *Yellow Pages* or on notice boards in health shops and health centres. Do also ask friends and family for personal recommendations.
- Make contact with your chosen practitioner before making an appointment to establish whether you think he/she can help you.
- Ensure that the practitioner you have chosen is fully qualified and a member of a recognised professional body with specific codes of practice. Does he/she have insurance to cover his/her actions as a healthcare practitioner?
- Many complementary therapies are now available on the NHS in the UK. Ask your GP if you can be referred.
- Remember to remain in control of any healthcare that you receive, whether it's allopathic or complementary.

AT A GLANCE: chronic fatigue

- Chronic fatigue, or feeling tired all the time, can be indicative of an underlying health problem, so it is important to talk to your health-care provider about how you feel.
- Fatigue, although frightening to experience when you are used to being a healthy and active person, is relatively common. You won't be the only person in your staffroom to be suffering at any one time, so take what comfort there is in that.
- It is possible to get over chronic fatigue, but you will need the support of your colleagues, family and friends. Communicate how you are feeling to them. Keep them involved.
- Consider using a gentle complementary therapy such as reflexology or homeopathy to help you to feel better about yourself and raise energy levels.
- Fatigue can see your energy levels fluctuate pretty widely. Some days you'll feel relatively fit, while others will see you totally drained. Recognise these fluctuations and remember that when your energy is low it will increase again.
- Take time off work if you need it. Working when chronically fatigued further depletes your reserves, and it is always best to take a day off sooner than a month off later. Listen to the signals your body sends while they are still subtle.
- Although you feel fatigued, it is important to plan an activity for each day even if you are off work. Slowly build up over time – remember, pacing is crucial here.
- Get good-quality sleep and aim to stick to regular bedtimes.
- Pay attention to your diet. The purer the food you eat, the less of a strain it will put on your body. Light meals, rich in fresh (organic) fruits and vegetables, eaten regularly throughout the day will help to even out your energy levels.
- Remember that there is opportunity in every situation. It may be a tremendous disruption to your life to be suffering from chronic fatigue, but there will be a positive benefit that you can draw from it. If nothing else, it is teaching you in a direct way about the way in which your body works.
- If you experience a setback in your recovery, just go with it. Forcing yourself to work against it will simply set you back even further.

- Remember that suffering from a bout of chronic fatigue is a clear indication that you need to adapt your working patterns so that they are more supportive to your physical and mental needs. Do not go back to your old way of doing things.

AT A GLANCE: classroom 'design' tips

- Advocates of tidiness often say that clutter and mess create a 'visual noise', capable of disturbing those that must exist and function within it. Keep your work and teaching space as clear and tidy as possible.
- Create at least one area in your room that can be a peaceful haven, even if this is just a corner with posters of peaceful scenes or a space with plants and perhaps a couple of chairs for quiet reading. Be creative; you know what will work for you and your pupils.
- Encourage your pupils to be as tidy as you (or tidier if necessary!). Your room should be spotless at the end of each lesson or session, and it is certainly worth asking children to spend a minute or two helping you to achieve this. By taking this approach, you are at least starting each lesson afresh, without the added negative stress of seeing old 'mess' around you.
- Is there one particular area of your work and teaching space that attracts clutter and mess? Why is this? Make the effort to reclaim this space and assign it a specific purpose, for example, make it into additional display space or a place for marked work to be put prior to handing back to pupils.
- Are there any draining colour clashes in your work and teaching space? Look into changing this, even if it means buying a tin of white paint. When you realise that aspects of your immediate environment are having a detrimental effect on you it's important to make changes.
- Be persistent when requesting that repairs to your work and teaching space are made.

AT A GLANCE: communication tips

- A classic cause of poor communication stems from people making assumptions that others see things in exactly the same way. This can be avoided if you listen fully to what others say and be honest about your point of view as often as possible. Contrary to popular belief, consensus is not always a good thing!

- Duck out of conversations that appear to be heading towards 'bickering'. It's easy for this to happen in high-stress situations but is unlikely to serve you well to be involved. Minor tensions can quickly escalate if left unchecked.
- Be aware of how easily some forms of communication can be misconstrued. Email can be particularly misleading, as can memos written in haste.
- If you have a disagreement, or even a stand-up row with someone, either at work or at home, be sure to take the time to reach a resolution. Don't leave disputes hanging, even if you agree to disagree or arrange to discuss things further at a mutually convenient time.

AT A GLANCE: de-junking tips

- If you have a desk, clear it at the end of each day. Do this with a religious fervour and you'll never face the end-of-term mountain of papers and trash that can so easily accumulate if left unchecked. It should only take a few moments each day.
- Deal with mail at the earliest opportunity. Never let your pigeonhole get jammed full.
- Look into home and office/classroom storage systems for your necessary schoolwork and administration. Organisation like this seems to have a beneficial effect on the mind, too! Don't forget to purge it on a regular basis.
- Store as much as you can on computer if at all possible. This way you'll avoid the need to maintain mountains of paper in storage. Do, however, back up everything you store on a computer. And back up your back-ups.

AT A GLANCE: fighting procrastination tips

- If you can't do a task immediately, don't put it off indefinitely. Give yourself a deadline for when you will either make a start on the job in question, delegate it or forget it. Make the decision; no turning back!

- Do *something* towards a daunting task as soon as you become aware that you are procrastinating. Once you have made a start, the job is immediately smaller.
- Procrastination will undoubtedly be at its worst when you are trying to work 'against the flow', in other words, at times when you are at your least productive. Get to know your inspired times and use these to the full. At your most depleted times of the day, grab a rest whenever possible. It's by far the most time-efficient thing to do in the long run.
- Remember how good you feel when a task has been completed. Relish this feeling!

AT A GLANCE: headlice

- Watch out for children who scratch vigorously, especially behind the ears and the nape of the neck where the hair tends to be thicker and warmer.
- If you think you may have caught headlice from a pupil (it's an occupational hazard!), using a nitcomb, comb your wet hair over a sheet of white paper. This may give you a clear indication of whether you have been infected, but it is not wholly fail-safe, so don't assume you are free of them if you find none in this way.
- Insecticide treatments are thought to be pretty ineffective, as well as potentially harmful, as the lice can become resistant to the chemicals.
- A relatively safe treatment method that many swear by is to apply an excessive amount of conditioner to the hair after washing it. Then, using a fine nitcomb, comb the hair thoroughly from the roots to the very tips in a systematic way, checking the comb after each sweep. The conditioner makes it impossible for the lice and nits to cling to the hair. Do this every other day for about two weeks for best results.
- Another method of cleansing is to wash hair in a basin of water to which lavender oil, lemon juice or vinegar has been added and then comb through as described above. Repeat often.
- If you find any live lice on your hair, then every member of your household should be treated.
- There are some homeopathic treatments available. A qualified practitioner will be able to advise. Likewise, a trip to your local healthstore may offer treatments that are alternatives to insecticides.

AT A GLANCE: meditation tips

- Consider joining a local meditation group while you learn the basics of what to do (or, rather, what not to do!).
- Don't feel that you have to devote hours to meditation. Obviously, the more you put into it, the more you'll get out of it, but it is most certainly possible to gain positive benefit from as little as ten minutes a day.
- Find a quiet place where you will be undisturbed. Sit in a comfortable position with nothing crossed. Relax as much as possible, while keeping your shoulders down and your back straight (not slouched in a chair).
- Close your eyes lightly and start to 'watch' what's happening in your mind. Thoughts will probably rush through it at alarming speed. It will take time to avoid this from happening but in the mean time don't attempt to stop them or solve problems. Just observe that they are there.
- If you find it difficult to meditate with your eyes shut, open them and focus on a single object such as a flower.
- Meditation is an art to be learned. If you cannot attend a local class, invest in one of the many fine meditation books on the market (see Further Reading).
- If you feel the need to take a meditative break at school but can't find a quiet space, just focus on your breathing. Take a pause, then a deep breath, then pause, breathe, pause, breathe until you feel calmer. Breathe from deep within, not just high up in your chest.

AT A GLANCE: motivation tips

- When changes need to be made, look forward and not back. Look at the possibilities of what the future may hold rather than at what hasn't materialised in the past.
- Set goals for yourself if you fear you might be 'drifting'. Make sure your goals are achievable and realistic and can be split into short-term and long-term desires.
- Do something, anything, today that moves you towards your goals. Take that first step, even if it is a small one. You'll be heading towards the person, or place, you want to be.
- Remember that you are entitled to live your life at your pace.

AT A GLANCE: nutritional guidelines

- Keep an eye on your portion sizes. According to the gym chain Esporta, the average daily calorie intake has risen from 1,854 calories to 2,002 over the last twenty years. This increase of 148 calories a day is enough to put on 15 pounds in a year.
- Aim to plan your meals as much as you can so that you have the appropriate ingredients to hand.
- Don't shop for food when you're really hungry – you'll be tempted by the wrong things.
- Don't take a hard line against any particular food group unless you have a philosophical or religious reason to (such as being a vegetarian or vegan). The watchword is moderation.
- Avoid fad diets, especially those that don't advocate a nutritional balance. We need a combination of carbohydrates and protein at every meal.
- Aim to eat frequently through the day. This can accelerate metabolism and ensure that you are fully energised throughout the day.
- Drink plenty of water. If you drink other fluids such as tea or coffee, make sure that this isn't to quench thirst but simply because you enjoy it. In other words, these drinks are *in addition to* your water intake.
- Consider taking a good-quality multivitamin/multimineral supplement. Go for organic if possible.
- Don't be too hard on yourself over food. It's far better that you are consistent in your approach to eating than extreme. Eat for the nutrition and energy it gives you, not for any emotional relief you may derive. If you suspect that your emotions may be entwined with your food choices, consider speaking to your chosen healthcare provider about this.

AT A GLANCE: optimism

- Is your glass half-full or half-empty? It's an unsophisticated analogy but still a useful one.
- What is your expectation in life? That things will turn out well or that setbacks and frustrations will ultimately rule in your life?

- Optimists take credit for good events and generally believe that the positive benefits they feel will be lasting and pervasive. Pessimists tend to blame external circumstances for what happens in their life and feel that, even if anything good does happen, it will only be temporary. Which are you? Optimistic or pessimistic?
- Psychological experiments have shown that helplessness can be learned, but can optimism be learned? Studies show that it can be.
- Become more self-observant. Catch your thoughts and replace self-defeating ones with positive and constructive ones.
- Be honest about your thoughts. When you evaluate them, how realistic are they? Do you ever make statements to yourself that are simply not true, or based on inaccurate suppositions?
- Be realistic about your life. The positives are there for the taking, so include them in your personal life-history.
- See yourself as a problem-solver in your life rather than the victim of events over which you feel you have no control.
- For one week jot down the positive things that happen in your life every day. After just a few days you'll start to get into the habit of actively recognising them as and when they take place.
- Align yourself with positive people. If there is anyone that you work with who has the potential to bring your mood down, distance yourself, or vow to 'protect' yourself from their pessimistic attitudes.
- Seek out the silver lining; it will be there!

AT A GLANCE: positive mental health

Dr Trevor Powell's book *Stress Free Living* (see Further Reading) suggests the following twelve steps to positive mental health:

- take responsibility for your own life
- be flexible in your thinking
- accept reality as a mixture of good and bad
- savour the moment
- learn to live with frustration
- accept and care for yourself
- express positive and negative feelings
- work towards goals

- think rationally and creatively
- manage your time and maintain a balance
- develop hobbies and absorbing interests
- develop and maintain relationships

AT A GLANCE: relaxation tips

- Taking time to recharge is essential, not a luxury. Make sure you know what will aid relaxation for you.
- At the start of each term, when you know the rhythm of what's ahead of you, such as when report times are, when parent consultation evenings are and when you'll be involved in extra-curricular activities, mark out 'holi-days' on your calendar. It doesn't matter what you do on these days, but it is absolutely essential that they are to be used for mini-holidays. NO WORK! Litter each term with as many of these special days as you can.
- On occasion, planning days when you know you will have to work late or put in extra hours can help to balance workload and ultimately lead to greater relaxation. If possible, look ahead to work out when these 'heavy' days are likely to fall and aim to follow them up with a 'holi-day' as soon as possible afterwards.
- If affording a holiday away from home is a difficulty, look at ways of budgeting for a break by saving even the smallest of sums over a period of time. Commit yourself to finding an opportunity to get right away.
- Work out what you can do close to home free or for little cost. Create a list that you can refer to when you want to treat yourself.
- Make something.
- Do something that appeals to your sense of fun and play.

AT A GLANCE: resilience tips

- Use affirmations to remind yourself why you teach. What brought you into the job and why are you still here?
- Take small incremental steps to improve your sense of well-being. Certainly, the big steps can help, but if you pay attention to the small ones all the time, results will definitely build up.

- As you respond to each situation, ask yourself: Is this an optimistic or a pessimistic response?
- Keep your work simple whenever possible.
- Think about how you can transform stressful situations. What can you draw out of them for your positive use? Can you diffuse them with humour, or simply remove yourself temporarily until you feel better able to deal with matters?
- Allow yourself to acknowledge the way you feel about things. Don't squash your emotions for being somehow wrong. Rather, express them through appropriate channels.
- Seek help and guidance when you feel you need it. This could come from many sources – for example, your school, your family and friends, a counsellor, a helpline, an Internet virtual staffroom such as that found at www.eteach.com and so on.
- Never lose sight of the fact that it is possible to take learning and meaning from every situation.
- Write a 'have done' list. Allow yourself a moment to relish your achievements.

AT A GLANCE: saying 'no'

- Just say it! It's not necessary to go into lengthy explanations or apologies; if you give a reasoned answer, that's justification enough.
- Keep calm in your response. You may feel annoyed at having been asked, but it's not always appropriate to express that.
- Be honest if you would find what you're being asked to do difficult to achieve. Perhaps suggest a compromise, for example, completing the task at a later date or to a different specification.
- Rehearse what you want to say. Script lines for yourself if you suspect you might give in when talking face to face.

AT A GLANCE: self-knowledge tips

- When you feel positive about any aspect of your life, make a mental (or physical) note of what it is that is inspiring this feeling. Revisit this information when you feel particularly low; it will help to restore feelings of well-being.

- Has there been a time in your life when you have wanted to make a change but not quite achieved it? What stopped you? Is there any reason why this would stop you in the future? What can you do to ensure that it doesn't?
- It is usually possible to derive some positive benefit from most, if not all, events and situations in our lives. This does not mean underplaying the importance or severity of life events, but does help us to glean as much as we possibly can from what happens to us. What can you take from an apparently negative event that happened to you today, no matter how small, that will serve you well in the future?
- Ask yourself on a regular basis: What are my drivers? For example, what impassions you? What inspires and motivates you? Keep your answers realistic and positive. Refer to them on a regular basis and vow to create more of these factors in your life.

AT A GLANCE: snacking tips

- Stock up on health-giving snacks so that you're not tempted to feast purely on fatty or sugary foods when you need a boost. Go for dried fruits, nuts and seeds, yoghurts or non-dairy alternatives, breadsticks, fruit and moderately sweetened cereal bars such as flapjacks and so on.
- If your school canteen offers the usual diet of stodge and additives, prepare your own lunches. Take a look down the well-being aisle of your local supermarket and you'll see healthy 'fast food' alternatives, free from additives, sugar and salt. If you make your own sandwiches, vary the bread you use and seek out a range of fillings that will inspire you.
- Aim to prepare a batch of freezable snacks so that you know you've always got a stock of healthy snacks to hand.
- Don't forget that a powerful way of avoiding blood-sugar fluctuations is to combine a carbohydrate with a first-class protein.

AT A GLANCE: standing and staring

- Grant yourself some thinking time. No one else can do this for you, so be firm about doing it for yourself.

- Take time to reflect, even if only for a second, before acting or reacting. Is what you are about to do supportive of your overall well-being?
- Consider the relationship between your creativity and the amount of time you spend thinking about your ideas before bringing them to fruition. Do you draw order from the chaos of thought or plunge straight in when you're not sure how things will turn out?
- Get some fresh air. Your brain may be only about 2 per cent of your bodyweight, but it demands around 25 per cent of the oxygen in your body.
- Make sure you experience silence for a period every day.
- Take a moment to ponder this Spanish proverb. OK, you may not get the chance very often to achieve it, but it's a goal worth pursuing. 'How beautiful it is to do nothing and then to rest afterwards.'
- Value your originality. Original thought is hard to come by, but the more you get into the habit of thinking, the more likely you are to experience original thought.
- Aim to find out when your premium thinking time occurs. Perhaps it's first thing in the morning or last thing at night? Or when you enter your 'thinking zone' (a physical space or a frame of mind). Is it during certain seasons, or at particular times of the month? Your creativity and originality of thought will fluctuate, so learn how to work with it.

AT A GLANCE: stress-busting tips

- Never forget to laugh. Remember that it's physically impossible for your body to be tense when you laugh. Even if this gives you just a moment or two of relief, it is worth it.
- Imagine a friend or loved one is in the situation you find yourself in. What objective advice would you give them?
- Feeling the symptoms of negative stress is fine. They are warning signals from your body and should not be overridden, suppressed or ignored.
- It is essential to create, and stick to, the habit of cutting off at some point at the end of each day. Do not return to work activities beyond this cut-off time.
- Have a 'no-bag day' at least once a week. Do not take work home on this day.
- Squeeze a stress ball when you feel tense or frustrated.

- The act of popping bubble wrap has, apparently, been scientifically proved to reduce stress – so, pop that wrap!
- When tackling paperwork, give your eyes a rest by gently cupping your palms over them so that they are in complete darkness. Just twenty seconds or so is all it takes.
- Keep a tissue in your pocket with a few drops of lavender oil on it. Inhale when you feel stress rising.
- Pay conscious awareness to your driving. Drop-grip the wheel like you're on a white-knuckle ride and drop your shoulders if they are hunched. What's your jaw doing? Release it if it's clenched.
- Avoid leaning on alcohol, caffeine and nicotine.
- Write down your feelings and all of the things on your mind. Once they are committed to paper, draw a line through anything that you cannot control. Now take steps to address what you do have some influence over.
- Pay attention to your diet. When your body's under stress it needs good-quality, highly nutritious food more than ever.
- Tap the centre of your chest rhythmically for about two minutes. Do it to a count of three, where the first tap is the heaviest.
- Tell your friends and family what you're going through. If you have children and/or a partner, it's particularly important that you communicate how you're feeling and why. Ask for support in the short run, but recognise that you cannot 'lean' indefinitely.

AT A GLANCE: taking time

Take time to:

- breathe
- celebrate success
- collaborate
- communicate
- declutter
- drink water
- eat
- exercise
- exhale
- inhale

- plan
- praise
- prioritise
- recover
- relax
- set goals
- show appreciation
- visualise
- write lists

AT A GLANCE: time-management tips

- The next time you are asked to take on an additional task, and an outright refusal seems inappropriate, be sure at least to ask for more time than you think you will need, not less. If you think it'll take you an hour, say you'll get it done in two. If you need a week, ask for three, and so on. This isn't unreasonable, merely realistic.
- Always use a diary or day-planner and get used to referring to it regularly. This way, important tasks and events won't pass you by and you will relieve your mind of the need to carry this information. It's probably best not to run two diaries (one for work and one for home) unless you know there's no chance you'll ever forget to look at one of them.
- For every task, ask yourself: Does this need to be done? If it does, do you need to do it or is there someone else you can delegate to?
- Live as close as you can to your school. Cutting down on travelling time allows you to regain 'you' time. It will also save valuable resources such as fuel and money.
- Delegate.
- Prioritise.

AT A GLANCE: transport tips

- Share your journey to work if possible. Not only is this good for the environment but you may also find that the inevitable work-centred conversations you have will help you to understand your colleagues and pupils a little more deep. Do remember, though, to have non-work conversations or you're simply extending your working day to include your travelling time.

- If you have to use public transport, there will be times when you feel out of control regarding delays. The positive side, though, is that you *cannot* be in control so may as well relax. Always keep a good book with you or a magazine that you know you'll enjoy dipping into.
- Always allow yourself more time than you think you'll need to get from A to B. If you're early, you'll always be able to fill the spare time, but being late will raise your levels of stress hormones.
- Aim to use your journey time to help you to distance yourself from work. You might not be able to wind down fully on your route home, but you will be able to shift the focus of your mind.

AT A GLANCE: vitality tips

- Physical activity can boost a sense of well-being, even through something as simple as walking a short journey rather than driving, or doing some physical exercise for relaxation.
- Stretching can give your energy an instant boost. Take a look at www.e-stretch.net or M Tobias and J P Sullivan's *The Complete Stretching Book* (see Further Reading) for more information.
- If you feel really sluggish at any time during the school day, splashing cold water on your face can be refreshing, as can holding your hands under a cold running tap, or dabbing your temples with cold water.
- Get outside as much as you can during your working day. Even if this means sticking your head outside for a few deep breaths in between dashing to use the photocopier and grabbing a drink in the staffroom, this will offer a degree of revitalisation.
- Don't forget to drink water, and plenty of it. Be proactive over this and don't wait to feel thirsty. It really is a life-giver and revitaliser.
- Only you will know how much sleep you need in order to feel good; it's just a question of making sure you get it! If you can go to bed at a regular time, you're more likely to fall asleep sooner rather than later. Aim to create good sleeping habits.
- Each morning, acknowledge the good/fun/exciting things that will happen during the day. However small these may be, the act of acknowledging them helps you to see that your life is not all work and drudgery.

- If you are the meal designer in your household, get into the habit of planning a few weeks ahead to avoid having to create on the spur of the moment.

AT A GLANCE: workplace harmony tips

- To a great degree, harmony at work is dependent upon those you work with. You cannot control their moods and grievances, but you can treat them as you would like to be treated yourself.
- Take the time to show an interest in your colleagues. Knowing just a little about their lives, and asking about how things are going for them, is greatly appreciated by most people.
- Celebrate together. Whether this is established festivals, birthdays, achievements, or just for the sake of it, never pass up the chance to celebrate!
- Be aware of when negative stress might affect the school, for example, around inspection time, exam time, report time and so on. Mark the end of it in a collective way, so that you can all draw a line under it.
- If you know that a colleague is under particular strain, suggest something you're comfortable doing to help out. Even if they don't take you up on your offer, the fact that you have asked will be a tremendous boost for them.

AT A GLANCE: well-being

Andy Mash, headteacher of a Norfolk First School in England and participant in the Well-being Programme, describes well-being in the context of his school as:

- looking after colleagues
- getting them to look after themselves by taking personal responsibility for their health and safety in the workplace
- managing the sensible expectations and demands made upon colleagues by others (as well as by themselves)
- exercising managerial responsibility for a 'duty of care'
- communicating

- maintaining self-esteem
- treating people fairly and ensuring equality of access to opportunities for training and development
- having a pleasant working environment that is safe and secure
- promoting healthy attitudes among colleagues
- receiving acknowledgement and appreciation for one's contributions
- knowing one's own typical behaviour and preferred style of working
- strengthening teamwork, collaboration and mutual respect
- recognising the causes of stress and knowing what to do about them
- distinguishing between appropriate pressures (positive stress) and negative stress
- spotting what causes unhealthy pressures upon people and how to respond to it

AT A GLANCE: books to initiate change

- *Flow: The classic work on how to achieve happiness*, Mihaly Csikszent-mihalyi (Rider). Introducing the phenomenon of 'flow' – a state of joy, creativity and total involvement. This book is an intelligent reminder that the way to happiness lies in 'mindful challenge'.
- *The Art of Being*, Erich Fromm (Constable). Perhaps this should be called 'The Art of Well-being'; it urges a way of living based on 'authentic self-awareness'. There's no 'easy awareness' here, or shortcuts to enlightenment. Fromm's concern is the art of functioning as a whole person.
- *Positive Thinking*, Vera Peiffer (Thorsons Element). Everything you have always wanted to know about positive thinking but were afraid to put into practice. Still a classic text.
- *Care of the Soul*, Thomas Moore (Thorsons). Tackling the evident 'loss of soul' that Moore perceived as a malady of the twentieth century, this explores wisdom about the soul with thoughtful eloquence.
- *The Healing Power of Illness*, Thorwald Dethlefsen (Vega). Challenging ideas about what illness actually is, this looks at the idea of symptoms being expressions of psychological conflicts. An inspiring alternative to traditional views of illness.

Some final thoughts

In three words I can sum up everything I've learned about life: *It goes on.*

(Robert Frost)

A book about well-being in the teaching profession could not be complete without acknowledging the fact that, although the organisational structures of, and personnel within, schools and colleges can greatly influence the levels of negative stress felt by individuals, only *you* can reduce the internal pressures that you feel, and only *you* can adapt your life to facilitate a greater sense of well-being. Nothing anyone, or anything, else does to reduce negative stress and enhance well-being will have any impact if there is not commitment from you to do your bit. The ability to control your well-being lies with you.

However, that's not to say that any experience of negative stress that you may have is necessarily your fault – far from it – or that you have to tackle anything alone. But it is essential to recognise and utilise the control that every one of us has to make our life more comfortable and less stressful. One step in the right direction is all it takes to start seeing results. The better you feel about this progress the more likely it is to continue.

Ultimately, we all could usefully identify what is 'bad' about our lives, in other words, the stuff we're unhappy about but that we have no control over and cannot change. Then we can look at what we can control and make changes to and what's great about our lives that we can do more of.

There may be occasions in your life when all attempts at reducing negative stress and enhancing well-being are futile. Nothing seems to work, and every ounce of your intuition and gut feeling is telling you to get out and do something else. The overriding rule in all of this has to be to listen to those kinds of feeling. If improving well-being would merely be papering over the cracks, don't do it. If what you really need is a change of school, or a change of career, even if only temporarily, then this will need to be faced. There is nothing to be gained from 'making good'; any positive results you feel from that can only be temporary, and the gritty issues affecting you deep down will still, eventually, clamour for attention.

Deciding to move on carries no shame whatsoever.

When facing negative stress, keep your eyes on the prize of who and what you'd truly like to be, but never lose sight of the fact that it's the small incremental changes that will get you there most efficiently through their cumulative effect. The pursuit of well-being cannot become a chore in itself, and you can guard against it deteriorating in this way by finding the rewards that exist in the events of each day, moment by moment.

Ultimately, well-being is about centring and balance. It's not about being poised on the edge of calamity and chaos, just the right side of negative stress, but about being firmly within sight of what all the dimensions of well-being mean to you. It is also about trust in your life's process, and about appreciating its extremes, whatever form they may take.

I wish you well.

Further Reading

There are hundreds of books out there on stress management and related issues. This is just a selection of those that seem most useful. If you have any suggestions for books that you think should be included, please email me: eh@elizabethholmes.co.uk

For overall background to the issue

Travers, C J and Cooper, C L (1996) *Teachers under Pressure: Stress in the teaching profession,* London: Routledge

Physical well-being

Barough, N (2003) *Walking for Fitness*, London: Dorling Kindersley
Budd, M and Budd, M (2003) *Eat to Beat Low Blood Sugar,* London: Thorsons
Chaitow, L (1998) *Natural Alternatives to Antibiotics*, London: Thorsons
MacEoin, B (2001) *Boost Your Immune System Naturally*, London: Carlton
Powell, Dr. T (2000) *Stress Free Living,* London: Dorling Kindersley
Sinatra, S T and Sinatra, J (2003) *Lower Your Blood Pressure in 8 Weeks*, London: Piatkus
Tobias, M and Sullivan, J P (1996) *The Complete Stretching Book,* London: Dorling Kindersley
Viagas, B Grant (2001) *Sleep: A natural guide,* London: The Women's Press

Emotional well-being

Denny, R (2001) *Communicate to Win,* London: Kogan Page
Estés, C Pinkola (1992) *Women Who Run with the Wolves,* London: Rider Books
Geary A (2001) *The Food and Mood Handbook,* London: Thorsons
Goleman, D (1998) *Working with Emotional Intelligence,* London: Bloomsbury
Olivier, S (0000) *101 Ways to Simplify Your Life*, Place: Publisher
Pert, C B (1997) *Molecules of Emotion,* London: Simon & Schuster

Rowe, D (1995) *Guide to Life,* London: HarperCollins

Sharp, P (2001) *Nurturing Emotional Literacy,* London: David Fulton

Stein, S and Book, H (2001) *The EQ Edge: Emotional intelligence and your success,* London: Kogan Page

Thase, M E and Lang, S S (2004) *Beating the Blues: New approaches to overcoming dysthymia and chronic mild depression,* New York: Oxford University Press

Townend, A (1993) *Developing Assertiveness,* London: Routledge

Mental and intellectual well-being

Alder, H (2002) *Boost Your Creative Intelligence,* London: Kogan Page

Boldt, L G (1993) *Zen and the Art of Making a Living,* London: Penguin Arkana

Craft, A (2000) *Continuing Professional Development*, London: RoutledgeFalmer

Forsyth, P (2003) *Successful Time Management,* London: Kogan Page

Grout, J and Perrin S (2002) *Kickstart Your Career,* Chichester: Wiley

Hindle, T (1998) *Manage Your Time,* London: Dorling Kindersley

Moon, J A (1999) *Reflection in Learning and Professional Development*, London: Kogan Page

Spiritual well-being

Bodhipaksa (2003) *Wildmind: A step-by-step Guide to Meditation,* Birmingham: Windhorse Publications

Goleman, D (2003) *Destructive Emotions: and how we can overcome them. A Dialogue with the Dalai Lama,* London: Bloomsbury

Goleman, D (1998) *Meditative Mind,* London: Thorsons

And for the sheer enjoyment of it . . .

Deakin, R (1999) *Waterlog: a swimmer's journey through Britain,* London: Vintage

Index

Figures and Tables in *Italic*